"It is a prison, ana the young girl is a king's daughter."
(See page 8.)

The King's Daughter

and

Other Stories for Girls

"WORDS FITLY SPOKEN"
Every Story Contains an Important Lesson

CHARACTER CLASSICS
VOLUME ONE

NASHVILLE BOOK COMPANY

Nashville, Tenn.   Marshall, Mich.

The stories in this book were complied from a four volume set titled, Sabbath Readings. The stories were orginally gathered from church papers in the 1870's, Methodists, Lutheran, Presbyterian, etc. We bring to you this 1910 reproduction, which is when the stories were first illustrated. We have found the stories to be truly "a breath of fresh air" in literature for children and youth. May they receive a warm welcome in your home is our prayer.

The Publishers.

Republished by:
A. B. Publishing, Inc.
Ithaca, Mi 48847

Cover Artist:
James Converse
COPYRIGHTED 1993 by:
A B Publishing

CONTENTS

ILLUSTRATIONS

THE KING'S DAUGHTER

I WISH I were a princess!"
Emma stood with the dust-brush in her hand, pausing on her way upstairs to her own pretty little white room, which she was required to put in order every day.

"Why, my child?" asked her mother.

"Because then I would never have to sweep and dust and make beds, but would have plenty of servants to do these things for me."

"That is a very foolish wish, my daughter, but even if you were a princess, I think you would find it best to learn how to do these things, so that you could do them in case of necessity."

"But it is never necessary for princesses to work."

"There my little girl proves her ignorence. If she will come to me after her work is done, I will show her a picture."

The little bedroom was at length put to rights, and Emma came to her mother, reminding her of her promise about the picture.

" What do you see, my child?" her mother asked, as she laid the picture before her daughter.

"I see a young girl with her dress fastened up, an apron on, and a broom in her hand."

"Can you tell me what kind of place she is in?"

"I do not know. There are walls and arches of stone, and a bare stone floor. I don't think it can be a pleasant place."

"No, it is not. It is a prison, and the young girl is a king's daughter."

" A king's daughter!"

"Yes; and her story is a very sad one."

"Please tell me about her."

"Many years ago the king of France was Louis XVI., and his wife was Marie Antoinette. They were not a wicked king and queen, but they were thoughtless and fond of pleasure.

"They forgot that it was their duty to look after the good of their people; so they spent money extravagantly in their own pleasures, while the whole nation was suffering.

"The people became dissatisfied; and when, finally, Louis and Marie Antoinette saw the mistake they had been making, and tried to change their conduct, it was too late.

"The people, urged on by their leaders, learned to hate their king and queen. They were taken, with their two children, and shut up in a prison called the Temple.

" There were dreadful times in France then, and every one who was suspected of being friendly to the king and his family was sent to prison and to the guillotine. The prisoners in the Temple passed the time as best they could.

"The king gave lessons to his son and daughter

Louis XVI and Family in the Temple Prison

every day, or read aloud to them all, while Marie Antoinette, Madame Elizabeth, and the young Marie Theresa sewed.

"After awhile the angry people took away the king and beheaded him. And shortly after the little son was separated from his mother, sister, and aunt, and shut up by himself in the charge of a cruel jailor.

"Next it was Marie Antoinette's turn to ascend the scaffold, which she did October 16, 1793. Her daughter, Marie Theresa, was then left alone with her aunt, the Madame Elizabeth.

"But it was not long she was allowed this companionship. Madame Elizabeth was taken away and beheaded, and then the poor young girl of sixteen was left entirely by herself in a dismal prison, guarded and waited on by brutal soldiers.

"For a year and a half she lived

Execution of Louis XVI

thus, leading the most wretched existence, and not knowing whether her mother and aunt were alive or dead. Years afterward, when she was free, she wrote about her life in prison. In that we read:—"'I only asked for the simple necessities of life, and these they often harshly refused me. I was, however, enabled to keep myself clean. I had at least soap and water, and I swept out my room every day.'

"So here in the picture you see a king's daughter, and the granddaughter of an empress (Marie Theresa of Austria, one of the most remarkable women in history), after having carefully made her toilet, sweeping the bare stone floor of her cell.

"Which do you think caused her the most satisfaction in those dark days of trial: the remembrance that she was the daughter of a king? or the knowledge of domestic duties, which she had probably learned while she was a happy, envied princess, living in a palace and surrounded by a great many servants!"

"Is that a true story?"

"Yes, Emma, every word of it; and there is much, much more that I cannot tell you now."

"What became of her at last?"

"She was finally released from prison, and sent to Austria to her mother's friends; but it was a full year after she reached Vienna before she smiled; and though she lived to be seventy years old, she never forgot the terrible sufferings of her prison life.

"But, my child, what I wish to teach you is, that though it is sometimes very pleasant to be a princess, it may be most unfortunate at other times. But always remember, my dear girl, that a knowledge of housekeeping never comes amiss, and every young woman, no matter what the circumstances are, will be far happier and more useful for possessing that knowledge."

Children do not always comprehend everything

at once; so I will not say that Emma soon learned
to take delight in dusting and sweeping. But bear
in mind that that woman is the most queenly, who
uses her wisdom and her strength for the benefit of
those around her, shrinking from no duty that she
should perform, but doing it cheerfully and well.

Queen Marie Antoinette Led to the Tribunal

THE OLD BROWN HOUSE

IT was very old, low-roofed, and weather-beaten, standing quite a little stretch from the road, and you might have supposed it deserted but for the thin column of smoke that wound slowly above the roof, so desolate did it look.

But it was inhabited, and could you have pushed aside the creaking door, you might have seen an old woman, wrinkled and gray, sitting by the silent hearth, stirring the dull fire, or looking absently from the window.

It was Aunt Ruth Jones, as the neighbors called her, of whom little was known, except that she was a queer old woman—a sort of hermit, living all alone in the neglected old house. It had come into her possession, with a small farm adjoining, by the death of her parents some thirty years before.

At first the neighbors were curious to see the new occupant; they found a tall, spare woman, then about thirty-four years of age, little given to gossip, shy, and cold. Some affirmed that she was proud, and others said that her life had been one of disappointment. But none had succeeded in drawing out her story, and gradually the old brown house and its occupant were left to themselves.

Years had wrought changes; the walls were now darkened with smoke, the windows dingy, the floor sunken in; there was nothing cheery in the ill-kept room, or in the face of Aunt Ruth. Some natures become shriveled and cramped when left to themselves, and hers was such an one; I am afraid it was also narrowed and hardened by being shut off from humanity, with none to share her joys or grief, or to care indeed, if she had any.

As the days came and went, they brought nothing to her but a little round of chores, a bit of patchwork, or straw braiding, and occasionally a walk to the village store to buy the few articles she required.

The gay dresses and pert stare of the village girls, the glimpses of happy homes caught through the windows, and the noisy stir of life, only made more striking the contrast of her own lonely lot. Gladly would she hasten back to her own silent fireside, where the cats, at least, were glad of her presence. Old Brindle knew her step, and tossed her head impatiently for nubbins of corn, or the pail of slop with which she was wont to be treated. The hens cackled merrily, and scarcely stirred from their tracks, as her dress brushed their shining feathers.

The care of these creatures was a kind of company, and on frosty mornings Aunt Ruth might be seen watching them eating so greedily, while her own breakfast was yet untasted, and her feet and fingers benumbed with cold.

Though none shared her heart or home, yet there was some-times one bright presence within those dim walls, a childish, questioning voice, and sweet laughter.

It was Bessie Lane. One June day, on her way to school, a sudden dash of rain had driven the child there for shelter. And ever since, the happy little girl, with flaxen hair and clear eyes, would go to the forsaken old house to chat with Aunt

"A sudden dash of rain had driven the child there for shelter."

Ruth. As that springing step was heard, and the latch lifted, there would come a gleam of brightness to the faded eyes, and a smile to the thin mouth.

The child found ready entrance to the lonely heart; children will, you know, they are so "queer," as wise old heads sometimes affirm.

"What in the world makes you visit that old hermit?" said Eliza Ray, her schoolmate, one morning. "Bridget, our hired girl, says she is sure such a looking old hag must be a witch."

"Witch or not, I like her;" and Bessie Lane tossed up her hat, and pranced off after a fox squirrel just down the road.

So Bessie kept up her visits, and the two would sit and talk together by the hour, Aunt Ruth showing her long-treasured trinkets, relics of years gone by, and detailing their history, till Bessie's eyes would dilate with wonder.

On this wintry morning, in which we have introduced her to you, sitting by the dull fire, and looking from the dingy window, the time of Bessie's absence had been longer than usual. The sky was leaden, and the wind whistled down the chimney and shook the casements.

Suddenly Aunt Ruth starts and peers through the window. There is a bright little hood and blue cloak approaching; she sees that, but not the carefully wrapped parcel Bessie is carrying, for she hurries to brighten the fire and brush the hearth.

"Good morning, Aunt Ruth. It has been ever so long since I have been here, has n't it?"

"Yes, a long time for a lonesome old body like me; but this is no place for the young and happy, I know."

"Oh, yes it is, dear Aunt Ruthie. You must not say so. I like to come real well. But Uncle Jake has been so sick; he sent for pa and ma, and I

went with them. It is such a long way off, I
thought we never would get there. And Oh, Aunt
Ruth, I have not told you yet"—and the chubby
face sobered.

"What is it, child?" picking up bits of litter-
ings from the floor. Somehow she always did so
when Bessie was around, the hands involuntarily
moved in little touches of order and neatness. The
room was good enough for her: for the child it
seemed dismal and must be brightened a little.
But Aunt Ruth was unconscious that she was
being called to a better life, or that a love for light
and beauty was awakening in her weary heart.

"Well, I will tell you; we are going to move
away. I declare, I think it's too bad to leave all
the girls just as I began to like them, and you, too,
Aunt Ruth. I don't want to go one bit;" tears
rolling down her face.

"Going away, my little girl going off?" said
Aunt Ruth seriously.

"Yes; and mamma said we couldn't move Chip,
it would be such a bother, so I have given poor
birdie away to Allie Smith;" tears flowing afresh.
"I let Amy Wells have my kitten, but I haven't
found a place for my poor little rose. See," said
Bessie, going to the table and removing the wrap-
per from her parcel, "isn't it a beauty? You will
keep it to remember me by, and take care of it
always, won't you, Aunt Ruth?"

The little blossoms were out in full, and seemed
to smile a benediction upon the old woman.

"Yes, yes, child, I will keep your rose; no harm shall come to it." The little plant seemed to carry her thoughts away, for she began talking absently to herself, then recalling her musings she said:—

"So you are going away; and you'll forget all about poor Aunt Ruth with so many new friends. Well, well, it's natural."

"No, no, indeed I shall not," said Bessie, giving her a hearty hug, "and sometime I will come to see you." They

"Yes, child, I will keep your rose."

talked a long time, but at last, with a good-by kiss to Aunt Ruth, and to the pet rose, she was gone like a flitting sunbeam.

Then the shadows seemed to come back to the inmate of the old house; but as her glance fell upon the little flower, she began clearing a place for it to stand in the warmest corner, musing to herself the while:—

"Just such roses I used to carry in my hand to
the old stone church in Amsden when no bigger
than Bessie. It seems like yesterday, but ah! it is
a long time. Maybe if I could do like that again,
it would not be so dark and lonesome like."
I think I'll put the rose here by the south window,

"It never looked quite so dirty before."

then if the child ever does come, she will see it
from the gate."

Bringing a little pine stand, she carefully placed
the plant upon it. In doing so, she chanced to
glance at the window. "Bless me! it never looked
quite so dirty before;" and Aunt Ruth moved
with new life, as she cleansed, rinsed, and polished
the glass. But this being done, the old muslin
curtain seemed dingier than common, shading the

clear glass; so it was taken down, and another finer one unpacked from a drawer and put in its place.

The next morning, as she ate her lonely breakfast, she placed her chair to face the window and the rose. The sun was shining, and as the rays streamed across the room to the opposite wall, she marked the cobwebs. That day the cobwebs were swept down, the other window washed, and the floor cleaned. The old house had not been so neat and cheery for many years.

Near the close of the week she went to the village, this time putting on a dark delaine, instead of the snuff calico with a yellow flower. Somehow the gay dresses and curious glances did not disturb her as much as usual. A pleasant recognition was passed with a neighbor whom she had not spoken to for a year.

A strange feeling had come over her,—a feeling that she was one of the great human family after all, and the icy mountain of reserve began to thaw just a little. Her purchases made, she concluded to take another road home. This route lay past a church. It was lighted, though early, and a few real worshipers had met to pray before the regular service.

They were singing now, and Aunt Ruth paused, as a clear, triumphant voice bore up the strain,—

"Plunged in a gulf of dark despair."

Spell-bound, she listened to its close, never stirring from her tracks till a group of people passed near, then slowly walking on, you might have heard her talking again to herself:—

"O Ruth Jones, where are you? I used to sing that, too, in the same old church where I carried the roses, only it was years after. I used to pray, too. I wonder if God would hear me now."

That night, and many nights after, she could not sleep; the words of song kept ringing in her ears, bringing up the old scenes and associations, till the great deep of her soul was broken up.

In her darkness she felt gropingly, feebly, for the old paths, and the good Spirit was all the time leading her back to the light. I can not retrace for you all the way that she came. I only know that gradually, surely, the night wore away, and the Sun of peace shone upon her soul. She went to the church, where the song had that night staid her footsteps, and listened to the words of life.

Her life became a blessing; for her nature was broadened, deepened and purified. The sick and needy learned to be glad at her coming, and little children ran to meet her.

And did Bessie Lane ever come again?

Yes, when June smiled upon the earth, the childish figure once more paused at the gate, but the blue eyes gazed bewildered around. "This is n't the place. Aunt Ruth must have moved away." Well might she think so; the house was neatly painted, the yard fence repaired, and up and down the path all sorts of flowers were blooming. Just

"Aunt Ruth must have moved away."

then Bessie descried a neatly dressed old lady tying
up some vines.

"Can you tell me where Aunt Ruth Jones has
gone that used to"
—Bessie stopped,
and with one bound
sprang into the
woman's arms, for it
was Aunt Ruth her-
self.

"It is so beautiful
here! how did it all
happen?" cried the
delighted child.

Aunt Ruth smiled
brightly, and, tak-
ing Bessie by the
hand, passed into
the neat, cheerful
room, and up to the
south window,
where the carefully
tended rose was putting forth beauty and fragrance.

"Bessie sprang into the woman's arms."

Bessie fairly danced with delight at sight of the
rose, but Aunt Ruth seated the child gently by her
side, and told how it had happened; how the little
flower had at first whispered to her heart of the
long ago; of the holy song that would not let her
sleep; and, lastly, of God's good Spirit that had so
tenderly led her straying steps to the sun-gilt path
of peace.

A STORY FOR SCHOOL GIRLS

IT was recess at Miss Capron's school. The girls stood together in one large group, talking very earnestly.

"I think it was a shame," said Marcia Lewis, "for her to make me face the corner for an hour, just because I spoke half a dozen words to Nellie Jones."

"I think so, too," chimed in a half a dozen other voices.

"She delights in showing her authority," said Lottie Barnes.

"So she does, or she would n't have kept Anna Mory and me on the recitation seat, for missing one or two questions in arithmetic."

"Do n't you think she is dreadfully cross? I guess if we should try to keep account of all her cross words and looks, we would have to be pretty busy."

"Would n't that be a nice idea? Let us make a mark on our slates every time she is cross, and see what a long string of marks we shall get."

"Oh yes ! let's do it ! Yes ! yes ! " chimed in a dozen voices in full chorus.

Poor Miss Capron ! With a sinking at her heart she saw the unloving looks in her scholars' faces as they entered the schoolroom after this stormy consultation. She had a severe headache that afternoon, so that, altogether, she did not wear nearly so smiling a face as usual ; and the girls, prejudiced as they were, found ample occasion for setting down their cross-marks.

Pretty soon Lottie Barnes held up her slate to view, displaying a long row of marks. Anna Mory imitated her example ; then Lottie Jones ; and in less than two minutes the whole school followed suit. This, of course, called for a reprimand from Miss Capron ; and then there was a terrible clicking of pencils. Soon Marcia Lewis dropped her slate on the floor, and the next instant every slate was on the floor.

"Girls ! girls ! " said Miss Capron sternly ; " you seem to have banded yourselves together to trample on the rules of order. I shall proceed no further with recitations until you have become quiet and orderly."

But even this seemed to fail of producing the desired result. The girls were quiet only a few minutes. Nellie Jones remembered that she had in her pocket a bottle of snuff for her grandmother, and in ten minutes the schoolroom was resounding with sneezes. Next, little paper balls began to fly mysteriously from all sides, and every girl appeared

intent upon her lesson. Presently, a half-sup-
pressed titter from Marcia Lewis awakened an answering one from Mattie Lee, and one after another
joined, until at length there was an almost deafen-
ing peal of laughter.

"The very spirit of mischief seems to have made
headquarters here this afternoon," said Miss Capron.
"It is useless to try to proceed with recitations,
while my whole attention is needed to keep you in
order. I will give you another recess of fifteen
minutes, and if you do not succeed in getting rid
of your excess of fun and frolic, I shall take very
prompt and decisive measures to help you."

The girls felt some little twinges of conscience,
but, after all, were quite delighted with the success
of their experiment.

"I tell you what it is," said Marcia Lewis, "Miss
Capron has no business to be so awful cross. Only
think what a sight of marks we got. Let's act just
as bad when we go into school again, and she will
have to dismiss us, and then we'll all go down to
the falls and have a nice time."

"Would'nt it be grand," said Nellie Jones.

"Splendid," replied Mattie Lee.

"Why! what is the matter?" said Mary Paine,
who had been absent from school during the day
until then and was surprised to find her usually
pleasant companions so excited. When she had
heard the whole story, she looked very sad : —

"Poor Miss Capron! How could you treat her
so!"

"It is just what she deserves for being so cross," said Lottie Barnes.

"Oh, you have been looking at the wrong side, girls. I have heard a story of a lady who began to find faults in her son's wife. The more she looked for them, the more she found, until she began to think her daugher-in-law the most disagreeable person in the world. She used to talk of her failings to a very dear friend.

"Finally, her friend said to her one day, 'No doubt Jane has her faults, and very disagreeable ones, but suppose for awhile you try to see what good qualities you can discover in her character. Really, I am very curious to know.'

"The good lady was a little offended at her friend's plain suggestion; but finally concluded to try it; and long before she had discovered half her good traits, she began to regard Jane as a perfect treasure. Now you have been doing just as this lady did, in looking for faults. Let us be like her the rest of the afternoon in looking for pleasant things. Let us see how many smiles we can get from Miss Capron."

Mary Paine was one of the oldest girls in the school. She gave the girls subjects for their compositions and helped them out of all their troubles. So being a favorite they consented, half reluctantly, to do as she said.

Miss Capron dreaded to ring the bell. The fifteen minutes passed, and she felt compelled to call her scholars. They entered in perfect order.

"She felt compelled to call her scholars."

Each took her seat quietly and began studying in real earnest. Frequently, however, a pleasant smile would seek an answering one from the teacher, and then one would be added to the rapidly increasing row of smile-marks. The good order and close application to study, and the winning looks, soon caused a continual smile to lighten Miss Capron's face, till the girls finally rubbed out the marks, saying it was of no use to try to keep account.

Marcia Lewis wrote on her slate, "It's smile all the time."

Before Miss Capron dismissed the school at night, she said :—

"My head ached sadly before recess, and I fear I was impatient with you. Your good conduct since has convinced me that I must have been in fault. I thank you, my dear girls, for your love and kindness, and hope you will forgive my faults as freely as I do yours. School is dismissed."

Instantly she was surrounded by all the girls and showered with kisses.

"We have been very wicked," said Marcia Lewis, "and it is not your fault at all."

Little Libbie Denny then related the whole story of the conspiracy, and when she told the part that Mary Paine had taken, Miss Capron put her arm about Mary, and kissing her, said, "Blessed are the peacemakers, for they shall be called the children of God."

"Well, my dears," she added, "which was best, looking for frowns or for smiles?"

"O, the smiles," said they all together.

"I wish you might learn a lesson from this, to remember all through your lives. Overlook the bad and seek for what is good in everybody; and so you will help to make both yourselves and others happier and better. What is the lesson, girls?"

And each voice responded, "We will overlook the bad, and seek only for what is good in those around us."

WHAT ONE LIE DID

IT was winter twilight. Shadows played about the room, while the rudy light flickered pleasantly between the ancient andirons.

A venerable old lady, whose hair time had silvered, but whose heart he had left fresh and young, sat musing in an armchair, drawn up closely by the fireside. Suddenly the door opened, and a little girl hurried to her side.

"Well, Bessie," said the old lady, laying her hand lovingly on the child's sunny ringlets, "have you had a good slide?"

"Beautiful, Aunt Ruth; and now won't you tell me one of your nice stories?"

Bessie was an only child, whose mother had just died. The little girl had come to visit her aunt, who had learned to love her dearly because of her winning ways and affectionate disposition.

But Aunt Ruth's eyes were of the clear sort, and she soon discovered that Bessie was not only careless about telling the truth, but that she displayed little sensitiveness when detected in a falsehood.

Now, if there was any one trait for which Aunt Ruth was particularly distinguished, it was her

The Spelling Class

unswerving truthfulness; and if there was any one
thing that annoyed her more than all others, it was
anything like falsehood.

"A liar shall not stand in my sight," was the
language of her heart, and so she determined, with
the help of God, to root out from her darling's
character the noxious weed, whatever effort it
might cost her. Of this she had been musing, and
her resolve was formed.

"Get your rocking-chair, dear, and come close
beside me;" and in a moment the child's blue
eyes were upturned to hers.

"I am old now, Bessie," and she tenderly stroked
that fair brow, "and my memory is failing. But I
can recall the time when I was a little dancing,
sunny-haired girl, like you. You open your eyes
wonderingly, but, if your life is spared, before you
know it, child, you will be an old lady like Aunt
Ruth.

"In those young days I was in a spelling-class,
at school, with a little girl named Amy, a sweet-
tempered, sensitive child, and a very good scholar.
She seemed disposed to cling to me, and I could
not well resist her loving friendship. Yet I did not
quite like her, because she often went above me in
the class, when, but for her, I should have stood at
the head.

"Poor Amy could not account for my occasional
coolness, for I was too proud to let her know the
reason. I had been a truthful child, Bessie, but
envy tempted me, and I yielded. I sometimes tried

to prejudice the other girls against Amy, and this was the beginning of my deceit. She was too timid to defend herself, and so I usually carried my point.

"One day our teacher gave out to us the word, *believe*. In her usual low voice, Amy spelt '*b-e-l-i-e-v-e, believe.*' Her teacher misunderstanding her said, quickly, 'Wrong — the next;' but turning to her again, asked, 'Did you not spell it *l-e-i-v-e?*'

"'No ma'am, I said *l-i-e-v-e.*'

"Miss R——, still in doubt, looking at me, inquired, 'You heard, Ruth; how was it?'

"A wicked thought occurred to me, — to disgrace her, and raise myself. Deliberately I uttered a gross falsehood, 'Amy said *l-c-i-v-e.*'

"The teacher turned toward Amy, who stood, silent, distressed and confounded by my accusation. Her flushed face and streaming eyes gave her the appearance of guilt.

"'Amy,' said her teacher sternly, 'I did not expect a lie from you. Go, now, to the foot of the class, and remember to remain after school.'

"I had triumphed, Bessie; Amy was disgraced, and I stood proudly at the head of my class, but I was not happy.

"When school was dismissed, I pretended to have lost something, and lingered in the hall. I heard the teacher say, —

"'Amy, come here,' and then I caught the light footsteps of the gentle child.

"'How could you tell that lie?'

"'Miss R—— I did not tell a lie,' but even as she denied it, I could see through the keyhole that in her grief at the charge, and her dread of punishment, she stood trembling like a culprit.

"'Hold out your hand.'

"There I stood, as if spellbound. Stroke after stroke of the hard ferule I heard fall upon the small white hand of the innocent child. You may well hide your eyes from me, Bessie. Oh, why did I not speak? Every stroke went to my heart, but I would not confess my sin, and so I stole softly from the door.

"Miss R—— I did not tell a lie."

"As I lingered on the way, Amy walked slowly along, with her books in one hand, while with the other she kept wiping away the tears, which would not yet cease to flow. Her sobs, seeming to come from a breaking heart, sank deep into my own.

"As she walked on, weeping, her foot stumbled, and she fell, and her books were scattered on the ground. I picked them up and handed them to her. Turning toward me her soft blue eyes swimming in tears, in the sweetest tones, she said,—

"'I thank you, Ruth.'

"It made my guilty heart beat faster, but I would not speak; so we went on silently together.

"When I reached home, I said to myself, 'what is the use, nobody knows it, and why should I be so miserable?' I resolved to throw off the hated burden, and, going into the pleasant parlor, I talked and laughed as if nothing were the matter. But the load on my poor heart only grew the heavier.

"I needed no one, Bessie, to reprove me for my cruel sin. The eye of God seemed consuming me. But the worse I felt, the gayer I seemed; and more than once I was checked for my boisterous mirth, while tears were struggling to escape.

"At length I went to my room. I could not pray, and so hurrying to bed, I resolutely shut my eyes. But sleep would not come to me. The ticking of the old clock in the hall seemed every moment to grow louder, as if reproaching me; and when it slowly told the hour of midnight, it smote upon my ear like a knell.

"I turned and turned upon my little pillow, but it was filled with thorns. Those sweet blue eyes, swimming in tears, were ever before me; the repeated strokes of the hard ferule kept sounding in my ears. At length, unable to endure it longer I left my bed, and sat down by the window. The noble elms stood peacefully in the moonlight, the penciled shadow of their spreading branches lying tremulously on the ground.

"The white fence, the graveled walks, the perfect quietness in which everything was wrapped, seemed to mock my restlessness, while the solemn midnight sky filled me with a sense of awe which I never felt before. Ah! Bessie, God was displeased with me, my conscience was burdened and uneasy, and I was wretched.

"As I turned from the window, my eyes rested on the snow-white coverlet of my little bed, a birthday gift from my mother. All her patient kindness, rushed upon my mind. I felt her dying hand upon my head. I listened once more to her trembling voice, as she fervently besought the blessing of heaven upon me:—

"'Oh, make her a truthful, holy child!'

"I tried to banish from my thoughts this last petition of my dying mother; but the more resolute was my purpose, the more distinctly did those pleading tones fall upon my heart, till, bowing upon the window, I wept convulsively. But tears, Bessie, could give me no relief.

"My agony became every moment more intense, till at length, I rushed, almost in terror, to my father's bedside.

"'Father! father!' but I could say no more. Tenderly putting his arm around me, he laid my throbbing head upon his bosom; and there he gently soothed me, till I could so far control my sobbing, as to explain its cause. Then how fervently did he plead with heaven, that his sinning child might be forgiven!

"'Dear father,' said I, 'will you go with me to-night to see poor Amy?'

"He answered, 'To-morrow morning, my child.'

"Dear Father, will you go with me to-night to see poor Amy?"

"Delay was torture; but striving to suppress my disappointment, I received my father's kiss and went back to my room. But slumber still fled from my weary eyelids.

"My longing to beg Amy's forgiveness amounted to frenzy; and after watching for the morning, for what seemed to me hours, my anguish became so intolerable that I fled once more to my father, and with tears streaming down my cheeks, I knelt by his side, beseeching him to go with me to Amy that moment; adding, in a whisper, 'She may die before she has forgiven me.' He laid his hand upon my burning cheek, and after a moment's thought, replied,

"'I will go with you, my child.'

"In a few moments we were on our way. As we approached Mrs. Sinclair's cottage, we perceived lights hurrying from one room to another. Shuddering with dread, I drew closer to my father. He softly opened the gate, and silently we passed through it.

"The doctor, who was just leaving the door, seemed greatly surprised to meet us there at that hour. Words cannot describe my feelings, when in answer to my father's inquiries, he told us that Amy was sick with brain fever.

"'Her mother tells me,' he continued, 'that she has not been well for several days, but that she was unwilling to remain from school. She came home yesterday afternoon, it seems, very unlike herself. She took no supper, but sat at the table silently, as if stupefied with grief.

"'Her mother tried every way to find out the cause of her sorrow ; but in vain. She went to bed with the same heart-broken appearance, and in less than an hour, I was summoned. In her delirium she has been calling upon her dear Ruth, beseeching you with the most mournful earnestness to pity and to save her.'

"Bessie, may you never know how his words pierced my heart !

"My earnest plea to see Amy just one minute, prevailed with her widowed mother. Kindly taking my hand—the murderer's—she led me to the sick chamber. As I looked on the sweet sufferer, all hope deserted me. The shadows of death were already on her forehead and her large blue eyes.

"Kneeling by her bed, in whispered words my heart pleaded, oh, so earnestly, for forgiveness. But, when I looked entreatingly toward her, in her delirious gaze there was no recognition. No, Bessie, I was never to be comforted by the assurance of her pardon.

"When I next saw Amy, she was asleep. The bright flush had faded from her cheek, whose marble paleness was shaded by her long eyelashes. Delirium had ceased, and the aching heart was still. That small, white hand, which had been held out tremblingly, to receive the blows of the harsh ferule, now lay lovingly folded within the other. Never again would tears flow from those gentle eyes, nor that bosom heave with sorrow. That sleep was the sleep of death!

"My grief was wilder, if not deeper, than that mother's of whose lost treasure I had robbed her. She forgave me; but I could not forgive myself. What a long, long winter followed. My sufferings threw me into a fever, and in my delirium I called continually upon Amy.

"But God listened to the prayers of my dear father, and raised me from this sickness. And when the light footsteps of spring were seen upon the green earth, and early flowers were springing up around the grave of Amy, for the first time, I was allowed to visit it.

"My head swam, as I read, lettered so carefully on the white tablet:—

"'AMY SINCLAIR,
Fell asleep September third.'

"Beside that fresh turf I knelt down, and offered, as I trust, the prayer of faith. I was there relieved, and strengthened too, Bessie," said Aunt Ruth, as she laid her hand tenderly upon that young head bowed down upon her lap.

Poor Bessie's tears had long been flowing, and now her grief seemed uncontrollable. Nor did her aunt attempt consolation; for she hoped there was a healing in that sorrow.

"Pray for me!" whispered Bessie, as, at length, looking up through her tears, she flung her arms about her aunt; and from a full heart Aunt Ruth prayed for the weeping child.

That scene was never forgotten by Bessie; for in that twilight hour, a light dawned upon her,

brighter than the morning. And, although it had
cost Aunt Ruth not a little to call up this dark
shadow from the past, yet she felt repaid a thousand-
fold for her sacrifice. For that sweet young face,
lovely as a May morning, but whose beauty had
been often marred by the workings of deceit and
falsehood, grew radiant in the clear light of that
truthful purpose which was then born in her soul.

TWO WAYS OF READING THE BIBLE.

W̱OULD you like another chapter, Lilian dear?" asked Kate Everard of the invalid cousin whom she had lately come from Hampshire to nurse.

"Not now, thanks; my head is tired," was the reply.

Kate closed her Bible with a feeling of slight disappointment. She knew that Lilian was slowly sinking under incurable disease, and what could be more suitable to the dying than constantly to be hearing the Bible read? Lilian might surely listen, if she were too weak to read for herself.

Kate was never easy in mind unless she perused at least two or three chapters daily, besides a portion of the Psalms; and she had several times gone through the whole Bible from beginning to end. And here was Lilian, whose days on earth might be few, tired with one short chapter!

"There must be something wrong here," thought Kate, who had never during her life kept her bed for one day through sickness. "It is a sad thing when the dying do not prize the word of God."

[43]

"Lilian," said she, trying to soften her naturally quick, sharp tones to gentleness, "I should think that now, when you are so ill, you would find special comfort in the Scriptures."

Lilian's languid eyes had closed, but she opened them, and fixing her soft, earnest gaze upon her cousin, replied, "I do—they are my support; I have been feeding on one verse all the morning."

"And what is that verse?" asked Kate.

"'Whom I shall see for myself,'" began Lilian slowly; but Kate cut her short—

"I know that verse perfectly—it is in Job; it comes just after 'I know that my Redeemer liveth;' the verse is, 'Whom I shall see for myself, and mine eyes shall behold, and not another.'"

"What do you understand by the expression 'not another'?" asked Lilian.

"Really, I have never particularly considered those words," answered Kate. "Have you found out any remarkable meaning in them?"

"They were a difficulty to me," replied the invalid, "till I happened to read that in the German Bible they are rendered a little differently; and then I searched in my own Bible, and found that the word in the margin of it, is like that in the German translation."

"I never look at the marginal references," said Kate, "though mine is a large Bible and has them."

"I find them such a help in comparing Scripture with Scripture," observed Lilian.

Kate was silent for several seconds. She had been careful to read daily a large portion from the Bible; but to "mark, learn, and inwardly digest it," she had never even thought of trying to do.

"Whom I shall see for myself."

In a more humble tone she now asked her cousin, "What is the word which is put in the margin of the Bible instead of 'another' in that difficult text?"

"*A stranger,*" replied Lilian; and then, clasping her hands, she repeated the whole passage on which her soul had been feeding with silent delight: "'Whom I shall see for myself, and mine eyes shall behold, and *not a stranger.*'

"O Kate," continued the dying girl, while unbidden tears rose to her eyes, "if you only knew what sweetness I have found in that verse all this morning while I have been in great bodily pain! I am in the Valley of the Shadow—I shall soon cross the dark river; I

know it: but He will be with mè, and 'not a
stranger.'   He is the Good Shepherd, and I know
His voice; a stranger would I not follow.

"Oh," continued Lilian, "in the glad resurrec-
tion morn, it is the Lord Jesus whom I shall behold
—my own Saviour, my own tried friend, and 'not
a stranger;' I shall at last see Him whom, not
having seen, I have loved."

Lilian closed her eyes again, and the large drops,
overflowing, fell down her pallid cheeks; she had
spoken too long for her strength, but her words
had not been spoken in vain.

"Lilian has drawn more comfort and profit from
one verse—nay, from three words in the Bible,
than I have drawn from the whole book," reflected
Kate.   "I have but read the Scriptures,—she has
searched them.   I have been like one floating carelessly over the surface of waters under which lie
pearls; Lilian has dived deep and made the treasure her own."

COURTESY TO STRANGERS

WHO was that quiet appearing girl that came into church quite late, last Sabbath?" I asked a a friend of mine who was an active member in the church which I had recently joined.

"Did she wear a striped shawl and a dark dress?" inquired my friend. "If so, it was Annie Linton, a girl who is a seamstress in Mr. Brown's shop."

"I did not notice her clothes in particular," I answered, "but her face attracted me; I should know it among a thousand faces. How could you pass by a stranger so indifferently, Mrs. Greyson? I expected that you would ask her to remain at Sabbath school, and go into your Bible class, but you did not once look at her."

"I did not once think of it, and if I had, probably she would not have accepted the invitation, as she is a stranger in town, and undoubtedly will not remain here long," my friend replied quickly, by way of defense.

I said nothing more, for Mrs. G. was really an excellent Christian woman, with this one fault—carelessness—which sometimes caused her to make grave mistakes.

But I could not help thinking about the stranger girl. Her large, dark eyes and finely formed face revealed more than ordinary intelligence, and in some way I gained the impression that, if not a Christian already, she desired to be. It seemed to me that she left the church very reluctantly, and was half waiting an invitation to the Bible class.

The next Sabbath she came again and occupied the same seat,—just in front of my own. She bowed her head very reverently during prayer, and once during the sermon I saw her lip quiver with emotion, and a tear came into her eye.

The services closed, and the stranger lingered as before. My friend, good Mrs. G., again forgot to speak to the girl. She passed out of the church slowly, and did not come again.

I thought she must have left town, as I had not seen her for several days; but one Sabbath, as I attended another church, I saw her again. She seemed a little more at ease, I thought, and there was a quiet smile on her face. After the services were concluded, I saw many a pleasant smile given to the stranger girl, and I understood the secret of the changed look upon her face. I made some inquiries, and learned that she had joined this church, and was earnest and active in all its work.

I also learned that she had made a profession of religion just before coming to our village, and had an unusually happy experience. How much the indifference of our own people had to do with her finding a home in another church, I know not.

Several years have passed since this occurred, but I have never forgotten it. Many a stranger's hand I have clasped, as I thought of Anna Linton's sweet face.

I was young in Christian experience then, and that lesson was a profitable one to me.

Speak to the stranger, Christian friend, with the assurance that God will bless your efforts to throw sunshine and cheer and welcome into the hearts of others—strangers though they be.

LIVE FOR SOMETHING

Live for something; be not idle—
   Look about thee for employ;
Sit not down to useless dreaming—
   Labor is the sweetest joy.
Folded hands are ever weary,
   Selfish hearts are never gay,
Life for thee has many duties —
   Live for something, while you may.

Scatter blessings in thy pathway!
   Gentle words and cheering smiles
Better are than gold and silver,
   With their grief-dispelling wiles.
As the pleasant sunshine falleth
   Ever on the grateful earth,
So let sympathy and kindness
   Gladden well the darkened hearth.

JENNIE BROWNING

THE light of a beautiful Sabbath was fast fading, and the last golden gleams fell softly upon the form of a light-haired little girl who sat by a cottage window, her head leaning upon her hand as if in deep thought.

The sun had departed like a grand old monarch, leaving behind him a glory of purple and gold more beautiful than his own full splendor. Yet the little girl saw nothing of all this beauty. She was thinking of the story in the Sabbath school book she had been reading,—the story of a child's life; and she wondered if all that happened in the story could be really true.

Jennie was pondering in her troubled brain a question which the reading of the book had brought. What could it be? Evidently it was not to be answered easily, for her face only grew more clouded, until at last she resolved to ask the help of some wiser mind.

Fortunately, Jennie knew that she had but to

make her perplexities known to her mother and they would all be explained in the clearest way; so, seating herself in her rocking-chair by her mother's side, she said:—

"Mamma, I want you to tell me something."

"Well, dear, what is it?"

"I've just finished my Sabbath school book, you know, and it's just perfectly lovely; all about the sweetest little girl; only she was always doing so many kind things for everybody; and I've been trying to think what's the reason little girls in books always have so many chances for doing good, and little girls like me, who are out of books, do n't have any at all."

"Not any at all?" questioned the mother. "Is that really so?"

"Well, no, not quite, I suppose," said Jennie, "but then they are just nothing but the tiniest little bits of things. There's never anything big and splendid for real little girls like me to do.

"Now, Susy Chrystie, in the story, took her little sister May out for a walk, and just while they were crossing a bridge, May pulled her hand away from Susy's, and tried to walk on the edge, just as close as she could; but in about one second her foot slipped, and she would have fallen off into the water if her sister had n't jumped right to her, and caught hold of her dress, and pulled her back all safe.

"Now just think, mamma," said Jennie, her blue eyes opening widely as she spoke, "Susy Chrystie saved her little sister's life; was n't that a splendid, big something to do?"

"Yes, my dear, that was a brave thing for a little girl to do, for even an older person might have been too frightened by seeing the danger May was in, to act quickly; but if my little Jennie will always try to keep quite still, and never scream when any sudden fright comes to her, she too may

"Susy Chrystie saved her little sister's life."

be able to think quickly of the best way in which to help herself or others."

"But, mamma, you know that nothing ever does happen to me; and besides, I have n't any little sister or brother."

"Never mind, my child, if you will do carefully everything you do understand, and obey cheerfully even when you cannot see why you should, you will please your heavenly Father and give me comfort and pleasure, and perhaps some day you may have a chance to do something brave."

Jennie's face grew brighter, as it always did when

she had confided her griefs to mamma, and for many days she watched and waited anxiously, thinking that at any time something might happen.

And so it did; for one day a letter came from Jennie's aunt, Mrs. Graham, saying she would come and spend a few days with her sister, and bring with her little Willie, a boy about two years old.

Of course they were very welcome, and Jennie greatly enjoyed playing with her cousin. He was a charming fellow, but very fond of having his own way; and one of his great enjoyments was to plunge two chubby

"He pulled Jennie's hair with all his might."

hands into Jennie's thick, light hair, and pull it with all his might.

Of course this was a short-lived pleasure when any older person saw him, but when they were alone, Jennie would endure the pain patiently until she could coax the little fellow to let go.

She never gave him a cross word, and when the

nurse would say impatiently, " Indade, thin, Miss
Jennie, it's a wonder ye do n't just shlap his
hands ! " she would answer gravely, " Oh, no, he's
so much littler than I am."

Yet Jennie was not perfect, and though she generally tried to do what was right, sometimes, like
the rest of the world, she wanted to do what she
knew was wrong.

One bright afternoon, when she was playing in
the yard, her mother called her :—

" Your aunt and I must ride to the station
directly, to meet uncle and your father, and I
would like to have you go quietly into the nursery
and sit there until Maggie returns from an errand;
it will not be long."

" But Willie is sound asleep, mamma, he does n't
want me," said Jennie, who was anxious to stay
out of doors.

" Yes, dear, I know it, but we shall feel safer to
have some one in the room, even if he is asleep;
something may happen if he is alone."

Jennie, however, was so unwilling to sit quietly
in the house that even these familiar words did not
attract her, but with slow steps and a sullen face,
she obeyed her mother's wishes.

She knew quite well how slight a thing she had
been asked to do, and although at another time she
would not have objected, just now, when she wanted
to do something else, it seemed very hard to give
up her own will.

Her conscience was so disagreeable, too, for it

would keep saying all the time, " I am ashamed of
you, Jennie Browning! Can't you do this for your
kind mamma, even if you do want to do something
else?" How tiresome it all was, and how she
wished she could "just do as she liked!"

Thoughts like these were filling Jennie's mind
as she stood looking out of the
nursery window; but all at once
she was aroused by the strong
smell of burning woolen.

Turning quickly, the child grew
almost rigid with fear as she saw,
just in front of her, a small flame
burst out from the rug before
the fire, and not far from the
crib where Willie
lay sleeping. In
an instant, how-
ever, the thought
" What shall I
do?" was fol-
lowed by the re-
membrance of
what her mother had often said, "If in any way
your dress should ever take fire, you must try to
smother it at once; never run away, but throw
yourself down, or wrap yourself in anything to be
found."

"*A small flame burst out from the rug.*"

Remembering this, she hastily caught up the
other end of the rug, which was large and heavy,
and threw it over the flame. This quite extin-

guished it, for it had only just started into life
when Jennie saw it; but in her zeal she tore off the
bedspread and blankets, crowning all with two
large pillows upon which she seated herself, for by
this time the child was so confused that she hardly
knew whether it was the rug or her
own dress which had taken fire.

Now she wanted to see somebody,
and, not daring to move, she began
to scream. This wakened Willie,
who added his voice to the
uproar, and soon
brought the be-
wildered nurse to
the rescue.

In less than an
hour the carriage
returned, and Jen-
nie was kissed
and praised more

" She piled on the blankets and sat on them."

than she had ever been in all her happy life, by her
parents and her aunt and uncle; for they saw
quickly what had happened, and trembled to think
what might have been.

That night as Mrs. Graham bent to give Jennie
her good-night kiss, she whispered, " May God
bless you, my thoughtful little niece, for you have
saved your cousin's life to-day ! "

" Why, did I really ? " thought Jennie; " how
glad, how glad I am; for if I had n't been there,

the fire would have caught the crib, and oh, that would have been awful ! "

Then, as memory brought the scene more clearly before her, and she recollected how her conscience had fairly pushed her into the room, her little face grew red with shame, and she softly said, " I will never fight with conscience again, for if I had had my own way, I could never have saved poor Willie's life."

PAST AND FUTURE

THE past is lost to us — the book is sealed,
    By mortal ne'er to be unclosed again ;
The past is gone — beyond all human power
To change the record of but one short hour,
    Though since repented of in tears and pain.

The future lies before us — a fair page,
    Whereon 'tis ours to write whate'er we will !
Then let us pause in case our careless hand
Shall make a stain which will forever stand,
    Through endless time a silent witness still.

'Tis not enough to keep the pages pure,
    And let them ever but a blank remain ;
Each leaf in turn should on its surface bear
Some writing that shall stand out clear and fair,
    To prove our lives have not been spent in vain.

ANNA'S DIFFICULTY

OUR friend Anna came home from school one day with her sunny face all in a cloud, and looking as if it might presently get a sprinkling of tears. There was one to whom she always went in trouble, besides that other One whom she tried never to forget, and she sought her best earthly friend now.

"Mother, I do think it is really mean and rude in the Wilsons that they pass me by when nearly all the class of girls are invited. I do n't want to feel bad about such a thing, but I can't help it. I do n't know as anybody likes to be slighted."

"Of course not, my daughter," said Mrs. Jones; "the feeling of having been rudely treated is always uncomfortable. What do you suppose is the reason you are not included in the party?"

"It is because the Wilsons feel above us, mother. The girls dress in finer clothes than I do, and have more accomplishments; and then we work for a living, and they do not. But, mother, I believe I am as intelligent and well-bred as they. I can't bear it, mother."

"It is not pleasant, to be sure, Anna; but think again, darling, before you say you *can not* bear it."

"Well, mother, who could? Nobody but you, who seem to have a way of getting round hard places, or walking through them."

"I have had many more years of experience in life than you. But I wish you to think now whether there is not some way for you to bear this little vexation."

"Oh, yes, mother, I know what you always say, and that, of course, is right; but I do n't see how feeling and acting like a Christian takes away one's natural feeling about being slighted and ill-treated by others."

"Perhaps it does not. I sometimes think one's sensibilities are greatly intensified by leading the better life. A Christian, in trying to bring his own character up to the point of perfect love and honor, often becomes exacting of such perfection in others, and failing to find it, feels exquisite pain. Yet the pain will oftener be because God's great principles of right are violated, than that his personal feelings are hurt. Which is easier for you, child, to be wounded in personal feeling, or to see what is wrong against God?"

"I never thought exactly; it is dreadful to see the wrong, but one feels in the other a sense of shame—feels so wronged—it is quite different."

"My precious one," said Mrs. Jones, "when you have so learned the love of God as to know no difference between the interests and the honor of his law, and your own comfort and pleasure and good name, you will see more clearly how this is, and feel, it is likely, the sense of shame and wrong in a different way."

"But, mother, have n't we a right to feel hurt when we are wronged or slighted — I mean personally hurt ? "

"Yes; but may be if we looked a little deeper into the principles of things, or our own principles, we should not suffer so much. What is the secret of your feeling hurt by the Wilsons? Does the slight make your real self in any respect less or worse? Does it injure you in the estimation of others?"

"Why no, mother, I suppose not; but I am as good and as much respected as they are; and I do n't like to have it seem that I am beneath them because I am not so rich, and all that."

"My dear, I believe we have talked this subject over before, and long ago understood that we desire no position, no companionship which is not ours by right of moral and intellectual character.

"It is the Christian principle to live in all things for the true and the right; to be willing to take our own place in business and society, and fill it well; to think less of what others think of us than of what we in ourselves are; to appear to be only what we are, and be willing to appear thus while we are always looking up to something wiser, and lovelier, and better.

"I never could get the idea of a Christian's being

above or beneath any one in the sense you mean. His associations are, or should be, such as Christ's were in His walk among men. Christ, infinitely endowed with all excellence and beauty, was also infinitely humble. He neither sought nor shunned any one for His own sake, but lived out the divine fullness of His life of suffering and love without regard to His position or popularity with men. I said He did not seek others, but I must except the beloved John, and the household at Bethany, and a few others whom He loved undoubtedly for their own sake, with a personal, human sort of attachment."

"You do n't mean, mother, that we should never seek people for their own sake or our own pleasure?"

"No, surely; but those only who are congenial in principles and life. Treat others with courtesy and generosity, and after that, allow them to be as indifferent to you as you are to those whom you do not prefer. Every person has a right to select his companions, and every one should possess enough personal dignity and generosity not to be offended if he is not preferred.

"I suspect you are wrong about the Wilson's. If they do not prefer you for your own sake, they have the right not to do so, and you should accord it to them just as you take the privilege of not inviting certain others who might feel the same about you as you do toward the Wilsons. And more than this, Anna; if the Wilsons live for different prin-

ciples, making friends for other reasons than you
do, why, indeed, should you care for their especial
regard? A friendship built upon the accidents of
fortune, distinction, or show, has but a sandy foundation at best.

"There is no security of happiness in any earthly
advantage. Only take care to be in yourself what
in your circumstances is noble and beautiful and
good, and you will find the right position without
any particular seeking. The love and approval of
the good and pure will come to you, and that is
what you want of any friendship, and nothing
more.

"Half the personal ill-feeling in the world comes
of people's aspiring to what they have no fitness
for; they have neither the dignity nor the humility to take the place God in His providence
assigns them; and instead of reaching out of it
by making themselves nobler and better, they
attempt to build up by some appearance which is
not more than half true.

"The real Christian will not want a name or a
reputation which he does not by right of goodness
or talent deserve; but by living well where he may
be, he makes any duty, any position, honorable and
good. He has nothing to do with the *false;* he
can afford to seem in all things what he is, and to
depend for love and favor on his consciousness of
worth."

"But, mother, I never thought of depending
upon anything else. The Wilsons know that I am

their equal in the school room, and in all the qualities which they ought to respect."

"You remember we spoke of a right of choice on
their part; and now are you, a Christian, going to
be hurt because fashionable people do not court
you? Can you not yet think of a way to bear the
vexation? Is it, in-
deed, so much of a
trial, as you think it
all over?

"You know, little
daughter, that Chris-
tians can look at
these things only in
the light the Christ-
life sheds on their
souls, on all their
earthly relations, on
the path that leads
them up to the
Source of light, truth
and right. Think
of it, and tell me to-

*"Well, Anna, have you come to a
conclusion?"*

morrow if you can bear to be slighted by the Wilsons."

* * * * * *

"Well, Anna," said Mrs. Jones the next day,
"have you come to a conclusion?"

"Really, mother," said Anna, "you have a great
way of taking the sting out of uncomfortable
things. I wonder if I shall ever get so as not to
care for my own sake."

"That will depend upon how closely you are united to God. If you live the true Christ-life, nothing of the sort will hurt you much; the consciousness of being right, the joy of His approval, will suffice you. But what about the Wilsons?"

"Why, mother, nothing about them; I don't think I shall feel bad any more. If they do not care for me, I shall not for them, only to be kind and polite; and I am sure I want no one's favor who does not love me for just what I am, and for trying to become better than I am. I shall go to school very happy to-day."

"I am truly glad, Anna; but always remember this: Every soul is created by the same God — purchased by the blood of the same Saviour, and has an individual life as dear to God as any other life.

"The Christian is peculiarly precious to Him, and however humble in this world's estimate, is an heir to His eternal glory and happiness; and so the Christian should, whatever may be his gifts or calling, possess that quietness and dignity of spirit, that, resting in the consciousness of God's love and approval, he will not be greatly moved by the applause or the displeasure of his fellows."

"And so, mother, it saves a great many uncomfortable feelings to be a Christian."

"It saves a great amount of disappointed pride and wounded vanity, gives many a sweet night's sleep in thinking God will take care of our reputation, being willing to be what and where He will have us to be.

"On the whole, Anna, it is a happier, more comfortable thing, for the relations even of this life, to be a Christian; not a half-way disciple, but a whole-heart-and-soul believer, who keeps no reserves to sting conscience with. He will not feel a thousand things that sting others; and the real troubles that he must bear are shared by Him who has promised to carry our human sorrows.

"Be at peace with God, dear child, and let the love which that peace brings, speak in the very tones of your voice, in your manners, and in your ways. Then you need not be embarrassed if duty calls you either to a palace or to a hovel."

"I shall get my lessons better to-day for that thought, mother. I shall not feel half so vexed if I fail when I have done the best I can."

"That is the intention of religion always, my child, to keep the possessor calm, assured, and quite aside from the little jostlings and vexations of a self-seeking life."

———

"THE past is written, the future is beyond our control, but to-day is ours, and is an opportunity to bestow a gift which will be more welcome than any that money can purchase. There should be no guesswork concerning affection; 'make it plain,' 'write it large.' 'Silence is golden' when it represses bitter words or ignorant comment, but it sinks like lead into the heart which has a right to expect tender and trustful utterances."

COMPANY MANNERS

WELL," said Bessie, very emphatically, "I think Russel Morton is the best boy there is, anyhow."

"Why so, pet?" I asked, settling myself in the midst of the busy group gathered around in the firelight.

"I can tell," interrupted Wilfred, "Bessie likes Russ because he is so polite."

"I do n't care, you may laugh," said frank little Bess; "that *is* the reason — at least, one of them. He's nice; he do n't stamp and hoot in the house, and he never says, 'Halloo Bess,' or laughs when I fall on the ice."

"Bessie wants company manners all of the time," said Wilfred. And Bell added: "We should all act grown up, if we wanted to suit her."

Dauntless Bessie made haste to retort. "Well, if growing up would make some folks more agreeable, it's a pity we can't hurry about it."

"Wilfred, what are company manners?" I questioned from the depths of my easy chair.

"Why—why—they're—it's *behaving*, you know, when folks are here, or we go a visiting."

"Company manners are good manners;" said Horace.

"O yes," answered I, meditating on it. "I see; manners that are *too* good — for mamma — but just right for Mrs. Jones."

"That's it," cried Bess.

"But let us talk it over a bit. Seriously, why should you be more polite to Mrs. Jones than to mamma? Do you love her better?"

"O my! no indeed," chorused the voices.

"Well, then, I don't see why Mrs. Jones should have all that's agreeable; why the hats should come off and the tones soften, and 'please,' and 'thank you,' and 'excuse me,' should abound in her house, and not in mamma's."

"Oh! that's very different."

"And mamma knows we mean all right. Besides, you are not fair, cousin; we were talking about boys and girls — not grown up people."

Thus my little audience assailed me, and I was forced to a change of base.

"Well, about boys and girls, then. Can not a boy be just as happy, if, like our friend Russel, he is gentle to the little girls, does n't pitch his little brother in the snow, and respects the rights of his cousins and intimate friends? It seems to me that politeness is just as suitable to the playground as the parlor."

"Oh, of course; if you'd have a fellow give up all fun," said Wilfred.

"My dear boy," said I, "that isn't what I want. Run, and jump, and shout as much as you please; skate, and slide, and snowball; but do it with politeness to other boys and girls, and I'll agree you shall find just as much fun in it.

"You sometimes say I pet Burke Holland more than any of my child-friends. Can I help it? For though he is lively and sometimes frolicsome, his manners are always good. You never see him with his chair tipped up, or his hat on in the house. He never pushes ahead of you to get first out of the room. If you are going out, he holds open the door; if

"It is Burke who brings a glass of water."

weary, it is Burke who brings a glass of water, places a chair, hands a fan, springs to pick up your handkerchief,—and all this without being told to do so, or interfering with his own gayety in the least.

"This attention isn't only given to me as the guest, or to Mrs. Jones when he visits her, but to mamma, Aunt Jenny, and little sister, just as carefully; at home, in school, or at play, there is always just so much guard against rudeness.

"His courtesy is not merely for state occasions, but it is like a well-fitting garment worn constantly. His manliness is genuine loving kindness. In fact, that is exactly what real politeness is; carefulness for others, and watchfulness over ourselves, lest our angles shall interfere with their comfort."

It is impossible for boys and girls to realize, until they have grown too old, easily to adopt new ones, how important it is to guard against contracting careless and awkward habits of speech and manners. Some very unwisely think it is not necessary to be so very particular about these things except when company is present. But this is a grave mistake, for coarseness will betray itself in spite of the most watchful care.

It is impossible to indulge in one form of speech, or have one set of manners at home, and another abroad, because in moments of confusion or bashfulness, such as every young person feels sometimes who is sensitive and modest, the every day mode of expression will discover itself.

It is not, however, merely because refinements of speech and grace of manners are pleasing to the sense, that our young friends are recommended to cultivate and practice them. Outward refinement of any kind reacts as it were on the character and makes it more sweet and gentle and lovable, and these are qualities that attract and draw about the possessor a host of kind friends.

CONFIDE IN MOTHER

THE moment a girl hides a secret from her mother, or has received a letter she dare not let her mother read, or has a friend of whom her mother does not know, she is in danger.

A secret is not a good thing for a girl to have. The fewer secrets that lie in the hearts of women at any age, the better. It is almost a test of purity. She who has none of her own is best and happiest.

In girlhood, hide nothing from your mother; do nothing that, if discovered by your mother, would make you blush. When you are married, never conceal anything from your husband. Never allow yourself to write a letter that he may not know all about, or to receive one which you are not quite willing that he should read.

Have no mysteries whatever. Tell those who are about you, where you go, and what you do,— those who have the right to know, I mean, of course.

A little secretiveness has set many a scandal afloat; and much as is said about women who tell too much, they are a great deal better off than the woman who tells too little.

The girl who frankly says to her mother, "I have been there, I met so-and-so. Such and such remarks were made, and this or that was done," will be sure to receive good advice and sympathy.

If all was right, no fault will be found. If the mother knows as the result of her greater experience, that something was improper or unsuitable, she will, if she is a Christian mother, kindly advise her daughter accordingly.

You may not always know, girls, just what is right or what is wrong,—for you are yet young and inexperienced. You can not be blamed for making little mistakes, but you will not be likely to go very far wrong, if from the first, you have no secrets from your mother.

To thy father and thy mother
  Honor, love, and reverence pay ;
This command, before all other,
  Must a Christian child obey.

Help me, Lord, in this sweet duty ;
  Guide me in Thy steps divine ;
Show me all the joy and beauty
  Of obedience such as thine.

Teach me how to please and gladden
  Those who toil and care for me ;
Many a grief their heart must sadden,
  Let me still their comfort be.

THEY TOOK ME IN

WHO is she?"

"Could n't say.   She is a stranger here, I think."

"Yes, she lives in that little house down by the bridge, you know, girls, that tiny bit of a house covered with that white rose."

"Where we always got such lots of flowers to decorate with because no one ever lived there. Why, the house is almost tumbled down.   How can anyone live there?"

"No one would if they were not very poor.   Of course you can tell by the girl's clothes that she is poor."

"Come on, girls, never mind talking about her," said one of the number impatiently.   "What difference does it make to us who she is?   We will be late," and the troop of merry girls passed on down the street.

Meantime the subject of this conversation was hurrying in another direction, her eyes blinded by the quick tears that had sprung unbidden to them

[72]

when the wistful glance she had cast at the girls
had been met with only those of cold curiosity.

"It is hard to be so alone," she murmured, "but
I must not let mamma know."

The girls went on their way, unconscious of the
wistful look, or unthinking that they had been in
any way unkind.

Nellie Ross had noticed, however, and she was
thoughtful all the afternoon. How must it feel,
she wondered, to be alone among strangers. As
they were returning home toward night, she whispered to her particular friend:—

"Do you know, Mabel, I can not help thinking
of that girl we met this morning."

"What girl?" asked Mabel Willis, with a
slightly puzzled air.

"Why, the one that Margaret said lived in the
little cottage you know."

"O yes. What about her?"

"Why she looked at us so wistfully, and I never
see her with anyone; she must be lonely."

"Well?"

"You know what the Bible says," slowly: "'I
was a stranger and ye took Me not in.' This girl
is a stranger and don't you think we might apply
that?"

"Just what are you thinking of, Nellie?"

"I was thinking that we might call on her and
ask her to join our Sabbath school class, and that
might open the way."

Mabel laughed. "You always were a regular

missionary, Nellie; but I hardly believe I care to
go with you," with a shrug of her shoulders.

Nellie was disappointed, but she said no more
for she had learned the uselessness of arguing with
Mabel, so she determined to make her call alone.

Nellie felt a little timid as she presented herself
at the tiny home the next afternoon. The girl her-

" 'I thank you, my dear,' said the woman."

self answered her rap, and invited her into the wee
living room. In an easy chair at one side of the
fireplace reclined a delicate, sweet-faced woman.

"My name is Nellie Ross, and I have noticed
you and thought you were a stranger here," began
Nellie in the winning way that had always won her
many friends, "and so I thought I would call and
ask you to join our Sabbath school class. We have
such good times, and Mrs. Allen, our teacher, is so
interesting."

"I would like to go," the girl faltered; "but they are all such strangers to me, and"—

"That will not matter," declared Nellie. "I will come for you and will introduce you to the rest of the girls."

"I thank you, my dear," said the woman, before the girl could answer again. "I am sure Edna will be glad to go. It has been rather a trying time for her, I fear, since we came here, although she has never complained, for fear it might worry me.

"She was always in church and Sabbath school work at home. But my health failed, and the physician said a winter here might save my ife.

"My husband could not come with me, for he must work at home to get money to pay our expenses, so Edna gave up her school and everything to come with me. We are compelled to live very cheaply, you see, but I am getting better, and I think I shall get quite well, if only Edna can be contented here," with a fond glance at her daughter.

"Of course, I shall be contented mamma," replied Edna.

"I'm sure she will like the Sabbath school very much," said Nellie, earnestly, "and I will come for her to-morrow."

She did so, and Edna went with her, although she felt a little shy, but the warm welcome given her by Mrs. Allen, and the friendliness of the girls, soon made her feel at home. It was not until the school joined in singing the last song, that she so far forgot herself as to join in the singing. Then the girls were astonished. She sang alto beautifully.

"Really," cried one of them as soon as they were dismissed, "you must join our young people's choir, will you? We do need an alto so badly."

From that time on, Edna had no cause for loneliness, for she was one of the girls, and her mother smiled and grew better.

———————

YOU will see the pools of stagnant water frozen through the winter, while the little running streams are bounding along between fringes of icy gems. Why is this? The streams have something else to do than to stand still and be frozen up. Be you like them. Keep your heart warm by feeling for others, and your powers active by work done in earnest.

JOHN HALL.

———

A HOUSE built on sand is in fair weather just as good as if built on a rock. A cobweb is as good as the mightiest chain cable where there is no strain on it. It is trial that proves one thing weak and another strong. BEECHER.

———

LITTLE self-denials, little honesties, little passing words of sympathy, little nameless acts of kindness, little silent victories over favorite temptations—these are the silent threads of gold which, when woven together, gleam out so brightly in the pattern of life that God approves. DEAN FARRAR.

" You were not here yesterday."

THE LITTLE SISTERS

YOU were not here yesterday," said the gentle teacher of the little village school, as she placed her hand kindly on the curly head of one of her pupils. It was recess time, but the little girl had not gone to frolic away the ten minutes, she had not even left her seat, but sat absorbed in a seemingly vain attempt to make herself mistress of an example in long division.

Her face and neck crimsoned at the remark of her teacher, but looking up, she seemed somewhat reassured by the kind glance that met her, and answered : —

"No, ma'am, I was not, but sister Nelly was."

"I remember there was a little girl who called herself Nelly Gray, who came in yesterday, but I did not know she was your sister. But why did you not come? You seem to love to study very much."

"It was not because I did n't want to," was the earnest answer, and then she paused and the deep flush again tinged her fair brow; "but," she continued after a moment of painful embarrassment, "mother can not spare both of us conveniently, and so we are going to take turns. I'm going to school one day, and sister the next, and to-night I'm to teach Nelly all I have learned to-day, and to-morrow night she will teach me all that she learns while here. It's the only way we can think of getting along, and we want to study very much, so that sometime we will be able to teach school ourselves, and take care of mother, because she has to work very hard to take care of us."

"The teacher sat down beside her and explained the rule."

"The teacher asked no more questions, but sat down beside her, and in a moment explained the rule over which she was puzzling her young brain, so that the hard example was easily finished.

"You would better go out and take the air a few moments; you have studied very hard to-day," said the teacher, as the little girl put aside the slate.

"I would rather not,—I might tear my dress,— I will stand by the window and watch the rest."

The dress was nothing but a cheap calico, but it

was neatly made and had never been washed. While looking at it, she remembered that during the whole previous fortnight, she had never seen her wear but that one dress. "She is a thoughtful little girl," said she to herself, "and does not want to made her mother any trouble. I wish I had more such scholars."

The next morning Mary was absent, but her sister occupied her seat. There was something so interesting in the two little sisters, the one eleven, and the other eighteen months younger, agreeing to attend school by turns, that the teacher noticed them very closely.

They were pretty faced children, of delicate forms, the elder with dark eyes and chestnut curls, the other with eyes like the sky of June, her white neck covered by a wealth of golden ringlets. The teacher noticed in both, the same close attention to their studies, and as Mary stayed indoors during recess, so did Nelly; and upon speaking to her as she had to her sister, she received the same answer, "I might tear my dress."

The reply caused Miss M——to notice the dress of her sister. She saw at once that it was of the same piece as Mary's, in fact, she became certain that it was the same dress. It did not fit quite so nicely on Nelly, and was too long for her, and she was evidently ill at ease when she noticed her teacher looking at the bright pink flowers that were so thickly set on the white ground.

The discovery was one that could not but interest

the teacher. Though short of means herself, that same night she purchased a dress of the same material for little Nelly, and made arrangements with the merchant to send it to her in such a way that the donor need never be known.

Very bright and happy looked Mary Gray on Friday morning, as she entered the school at an early hour. She waited only to place her books in neat order in her desk, ere she approached the teacher, and whispering in a voice that laughed in spite of her efforts to make it low and deferential.

"After this week sister Nelly is coming to school every day, and oh, I am so glad!"

"That is very good news," replied the teacher kindly. "Nelly is fond of her books, I.see, and I am happy to know that she can have an opportunity to study them every day."

Then she continued, a little good-natured mischief in her eyes,—"But can your mother spare you both conveniently?"

"Oh, yes, ma'am, yes ma'am, she can now. Something happened that she didn't expect, and she is as glad to have us come as we are to do so." She hesitated a moment, but her young heart was filled to the brim with joy, and when a child is happy, it is as natural to tell the cause as it is for a bird to warble when the sun shines. So out of the fullness of her heart she spoke and told her teacher this little story:—

She and her sister were the only children of a poor widow, whose health was so delicate that it was almost impossible to support herself and daughters. She was obliged to keep them out of school all winter, as they had no suitable clothes to wear, but she told them that if they could earn enough to buy each of them a new dress, by doing odd chores for the neighbors, they might go in the spring.

Very earnestly had the little girls improved their stray chances, and very carefully hoarded the copper coins which usually repaid them. They had nearly saved enough to buy a dress, when Nelly was taken sick, and as the mother had no money beforehand, poor Nelly's money had to be used for medicine.

"Oh, I did feel so bad when school opened and Nelly could not go, because she had no dress," said Mary. "I told mother I would n't go either, but she said I would better, for I could teach sister some, and it would be better than no schooling.

"I stood it for a fortnight, but Nelly's little face seemed all the time looking at me on the way to school, and I could n't be happy a bit, so I finally thought of a way by which we could both go. I told mother I would come one day, and the next I would lend Nelly my dress and she might come; that's the way we have done this week. But last night, do n't you think, somebody sent sister a dress just like mine, and now she can come too.

"Oh, if I only knew who it was, I would get down on my knees and thank them, and so would Nelly. But we do n't know, and so we've done all we could for them,— we've prayed for them,— and Oh, Miss M——, we are all so glad now. Aren't you too?"

"Indeed I am," was the emphatic answer.

The following Monday, little Nelly, in the new pink dress, entered the schoolroom with her sister. Her face was as radiant as a rose in sunshine, and approaching the teacher's table, she exclaimed:—

"I am coming to school every day, and oh, I am so glad!"

The teacher felt as she had never done before, that it is "more blessed to give than to receive." No millionaire, when he saw his name in public prints, lauded for his thousand dollar charities, was ever so happy as the poor school-teacher who wore her gloves half a summer longer than she ought, and thereby saved enough to buy that little fatherless girl a calico dress.

"Nellie entered the schoolroom with her sister."

A VALUABLE SECRET

"SARAH, I wish you would lend me your thimble. I can never find mine when I want it."

"Why can not you find it, Mary?"

"If you do not choose to lend me yours, I can borrow of somebody else."

"I am willing to lend it to you, Mary. Here it is."

"I knew you would let me have it."

"Why do you always come to me to borrow when you have lost anything, Mary?"

"Because you never lose your things, and always know where to find them."

"How do you suppose I always know where to find my things?"

"I am sure I cannot tell. If I knew, I might, perhaps, sometimes contrive to find my own."

"This is the secret. I have a place for everything, and after I have done using anything, it is my rule to put it away in its proper place."

"Yes, just as though your life depended upon it."

"My life does not depend upon it, Mary, but my convenience does very much."

"Well, I never can find time to put my things away."

"How much more time will it take to put a thing away in its proper place, than it will be to hunt after it, when it is lost?"

"Well, I'll never borrow of you again, you may depend on it."

"Why? you are not offended, Mary, I hope!"

"Oh no, Sarah. But I am ashamed that I have been so careless and disorderly, and now resolve to do as you do, to have a place for everything, and everything in its place."

"Well, Mary, this is a good resolution and will be easily carried out, if you bear in mind that, 'Heaven's first law is order.'"

TRUE worth is in *being*, not *seeming* —
 In doing each day that goes by
Some little good — not in the dreaming
 Of great things to do by-and-by.

We cannot make bargains for blisses,
 Nor catch them, like fishes, in nets;
And sometimes the thing our life misses
 Helps more than the good that it gets.

" What I can't tell mother, is not fit for me to know."

TELLING MOTHER

A GROUP of young girls stood about the door of the schoolroom one afternoon, whispering together, when a little girl joined them, and asked what they were doing.

"I am telling the girls a secret, Kate, and we will let you know, if you will promise not to tell any one as long as you live," was the reply.

"I won't tell any one but my mother," replied Kate. "I tell her everything, for she is my best friend."

"No, not even your mother, no one in the world."

"Well, then I can't hear it; for what I can't tell mother, is not fit for me to know."

After speaking these words, Kate walked away slowly, and perhaps sadly, yet with a quiet conscience, while her companions went on with their secret conversation.

I am sure that if Kate continued to act on that principle, she became a virtuous, useful woman. No child of a Christian mother will be likely to take a sinful course, if Kate's reply is taken for a rule of conduct.

As soon as a boy listens to conversations at school or on the playground, which he would fear or blush to repeat to his mother, he is in the way of temptation, and no one can tell where he will stop. Many a man dying in disgrace, in prison, or on the scaffold, has looked back with bitter remorse to the time when he first listened to a sinful companion who came between him and a pious mother.

Girls, if you would be respected and honored in this life and form characters for heaven, make Kate's reply your rule : —

"*What I cannot tell my mother is unfit for me to know.*" No other person can have as great an interest in your welfare and prosperity as a true, Christian mother.

Every girl should always remember that a Christian mother is her best earthly friend, from whom no secret should be kept.

————

HIGHEST aim and true endeavor ;
    Earnest work, with patient might ;
Hoping, trusting, singing ever ;
    Battling bravely for the right ;
Loving God, all men forgiving ;
    Helping weaker feet to stand, —
These will make a life worth living,
    Make it noble, make it grand.

A STORY OF SCHOOL LIFE

OH, girls! I shall just die, I know I shall!" exclaimed Belle Burnette, going off into a hysterical fit of laughter, which she vainly pretended to smother behind an elegant lace edged handkerchief.

"What is it, you provoking thing! Why don't you tell us, so we can laugh too?"

"Well—you—see," she gasped out at last, "we've got a new pupil—the queerest looking thing you ever saw. I happened to be in madam's room when she came. She came in the stage, and had a mite of an old-fashioned hair trunk, not much bigger than a band-box, and she came into madam's room with a funny little basket in her hand, and sat down as if she had come to stay forever.

"'Are you Madam Gazin?' she asked.

"'Yes,' replied the teacher, 'that is my name.'

"'Well, I've come to stay a year at your school.'

"And then she pulled a handkerchief out of her basket, and unrolled it till she found an old leather

[87]

"That is just the amount, I believe.'

wallet, and actually took out $250 and laid it in
madam's hand, as she said : —

"That is just the amount, I believe; will you
please give me a receipt for it ? '

"You never saw madam look so surprised. She
actually did n't know what to say for a minute, but
she gave her the receipt, asked a few more
questions, and had her taken to No. 10, and there
she is now, this very minute."

"Well, what was there so funny about all that?"

"Why, this: she has red hair, tucked into a
black net, and looks just like a fright, every way.
She had on a brown delaine dress, without a sign
of a ruffle, or trimming of any kind, and the shab-
biest hat and shawl you ever saw. You'll laugh,
too, when you see her."

Belle Burnette was an only child, and her
wealthy father was pleased to gratify her every
whim. So, besides being far too elegantly dressed
for a schoolgirl, she was supplied with plenty of
pocket money, and being very generous and full of
life and fun, she was the acknowledged leader
among madam's pupils.

When the tea bell rang, the new-comer was
escorted to the dining-room, and introduced to her
schoolmates as Miss Fannie Comstock. She had
exchanged her brown delaine for a plain, calico
dress, with a bit of white edging about the neck.

She did look rather queer, with her small, thin,
freckled face, and her red hair brushed straight
back from her face, and hidden as much as possible

under a large, black net, and but for the presence
of madam, her first reception would have been ex-
ceedingly unpleasant. She was shy and awkward,
and evidently ill at ease among so many strangers.

As soon as possible, she hastened back to the se-
clusion of her own room. The next day she was
examined, and assigned to her place in the different
classes, and to the surprise of all, she was far in
advance of those of her age.

But this did not awaken the respect of her
schoolmates as it should have done. On the con-
trary, Belle Burnette and her special friends were
highly indignant about it, and at once began a
series of petty annoyances, whenever it was safe to
do so. This kept poor Fannie miserable, indeed,
although she seemed to take no notice of it.

A few weeks passed by. Her lessons were
always perfectly recited. She made no complaint
of the slights and sneers of her companions, but
kept out of their way as much as possible. Her
thin face grew paler, however, and there were dark
rings about her eyes. A watchful friend would
have seen that all these things were wearing cruelly
upon her young life.

One day the very spirit of wickedness seemed let
loose among the girls. Madam was away, and the
other teachers were busy in their rooms. Fannie
had been out for a walk and was near the door of
her room, when a dozen or more of the girls surrounded her, clasping hands together so she was a
prisoner in their midst.

For a moment she begged piteously to be released, but they only laughed the more, and began walking around and around, singing something which Belle had composed,—cruel, miserable, insulting words.

She stood for an instant, pale and still, then, with a piercing cry, she burst through the ring, rushed

"She begged piteously to be released."

into her own room, closed and locked the door. Through their wild peals of laughter, the girls heard a strange moan and a heavy fall.

"I believe she has fainted," said Belle.

"What shall we do?" questioned another.

For a moment they stood there sober enough; then one of them ran for the matron, and told her that Fanny Comstock had fainted in her room, and that the door was locked.

The matron ordered a long ladder put to the window, and sent the janitor to see if it was true. Fortunately the window was open, and in a few moments he had unlocked the door from the inside. The girls were huddled together in a frightened group, while madam lifted the poor girl and laid her upon her bed. She was in violent spasms.

The doctor was sent for, but when the spasms ceased, alarming symptoms set in, and he pronounced it a serious case of brain fever. It is impossible to tell the shame and remorse of the conscience-stricken girls.

They were not brave enough to confess their guilt, but hung around the sick room offering their services, vainly wishing that they might atone for it in some way. But their presence only excited the poor sufferer, so that they were all sent away.

Day after day passed, and still the young sufferer raved in violent delirium.

But amid all her wild ravings not a word of complaint at the ill treatment she had received ever escaped her lips.

The little hair trunk was searched to find some clue to her friends, but there was nothing found in it but the plainest, scantiest supply of clothes.

Day after day the doctor came, looking grave and anxious, and at last the crisis came. For many hours she lay as if dead, and not a sound was permitted to disturb the silence, while anxious watchers waited to see whether she would live or die.

At last she opened her eyes; and the suspense was relieved by an assuring word from the doctor, that with careful nursing she would soon be well again. But her convalescence was slow and tedious.

Her former tormentors dared not even yet show the true courage to confess what they had done, but they daily sent little bouquets of fragrant flowers and many delicacies to tempt her returning appetite. Her eyes would light up with surprise and pleasure at the little gifts.

One day madam was sitting by her side, and as

In the Sick Room

Fanny seemed to be much stronger, she ventured to ask after her friends.

"I have no friends, madam, only cousin John who has a large family of his own, and has never cared for me. Mother died when I was born. I had a step-mother, but father died five years after, and I've taken care of myself ever since."

"And you are only fifteen now?"

"Yes, ma'am."

"How did you get money enough to pay for a year's board and tuition here?"

"I earned it all, madam, every cent of it. As soon as I was big enough I went into a factory, and earned two dollars a week at first, and

"I used to fix a book open on my loom."

finally three dollars and a half;
and I worked for my board nights and mornings."

"Poor child!"

"Oh no, ma'am, I was very glad to do it."

"But how did you keep along so well with your studies?"

"I used to fix a book open on my loom, where I could catch a sentence now and then, and the overseer did not object, because I always did my work well. You see, madam, I wanted to be a teacher sometime, and I'd have a better chance to learn here than anywhere else, so I determined to do it."

"What are your plans for the long vacation?"

"I must go back to the factory and earn enough to get some warmer clothes for the winter. You see, madam, why I can't afford to dress better."

Madam's heart was full. She bent over the white, thin, little face, and kissed it reverently.

That evening, when the girls gathered in the chapel for worship, she told Fannie's story. There was not a dry eye in the room. The moment madam finished, Belle Burnette sprang up with the tears coursing down her cheeks, and said:—

"Oh, madam! We have been awfully cruel and wicked to that poor girl. We have made fun of her from the first, and she would not have been sick as she was if we had not tormented her almost to death. I was the most to blame.

"It was I that led on the rest, and we have suffered terribly all these weeks, fearing she might die. You may expel me, or punish me in any way you please; for I deserve it; and I shall go down on my knees to ask her pardon, as soon as you will let me see her."

"My child, I am shocked to hear this. I can scarcely believe that any of my pupils would ill-treat a companion because she was so unfortunate as to be plain and poor. But you have made a noble confession, and I forgive you as freely as I

believe she will, when she knows how truly you
have repented of your unkindness."

By degrees, as she was able to bear it, one after
another went to Fannie and begged her forgiveness, which was freely granted. She said:—

"I do n't wonder you made fun of me. I know
I was poorly dressed, and awful homely. I would
have pulled every hair out of my head long ago
only I knew it would grow out as red as ever. But,
oh! if I could have felt that I had just one friend
among you all I could have borne it; but somehow it
just broke my heart to have you all turn against me."

After this she gained rapidly, and one fine morning the doctor said she might join the girls in the
drawing room for an hour before tea. There had
been a vast deal of whispering and hurrying to and
fro of late, among the girls, of which Fannie had
been totally unconscious.

At the appointed time, madam herself came to
assist her, and leaning upon her strong arm, the
young girl walked feebly through the long hall and
down the stairs.

"My dear, the girls have planned a little surprise
for you, to make the hour as pleasant as possible."

She opened the door and seated Fannie in an
easy chair, as the girls came gliding in, with
smiling faces, singing a sweet song of welcome.
At its close Belle Burnette approached and placed
a beautiful wreath of flowers upon her head,
saying:—

"Dear Fannie, we crown you our queen to-day,

knowing well how far above us all you are in His
sight, who looketh upon the heart instead of the
outward appearance. You have taught us a lesson
we shall never forget, and we beg you to accept a
token of sincere love and repentance for our treatment of you in the past, which you will find in
your room on your return."

Fannie's eyes were full of tears, and she tried to
say a word in reply, but madam spoke for her, and
after another song, they followed their newly
crowned queen to the dining-room, where a most
tempting feast was laid in honor of the occasion.

Fannie was quietly, tearfully happy through it
all, yet so wearied with the unusual excitement
that madam said she must not see the girl's "peace
offering" that night.

The first thing she saw the next morning was a
fine large trunk, and lying upon it a card: "For
Miss Fannie Comstock, from her teacher and
schoolmates." Opening it, she saw that it was
packed full of newly folded garments, but she had no
time to examine the contents until after breakfast,
when they left her alone with her wonderful gifts.

There were pretty dresses and sacques, a fine new
parasol, gloves and ribbons, cuffs and collars in
abundance — indeed, everything that a young
schoolgirl could possibly need. Every one of
madam's two hundred and ten pupils had con-
tributed from their choicest and best, to furnish a
complete outfit for their less favored mate.

"On the floor, crying like a baby."

At the bottom was a well-filled writing desk, an album containing all their pictures, and a pretty purse containing $5, and the following note from madam : —

"MY DEAR CHILD: This shall be a receipt in full for all expenses, during whatever time you may choose to remain in the seminary. This I present you as a sincere token of my love and respect.
                                    "JEANNETTE GAZIN."

They found her at dinner time on the floor, surrounded by her new treasures, crying like a baby; but it did her good. She was soon able to begin her studies once more, and was ever afterward treated with kindness and consideration, even though all her hair came out and left her head bald as her face, so that she had to wear a queer cap-like wig for many weeks.

When the long vacation arrived, Belle carried her off to her beautiful home on the Hudson, where for the first time in her life she was surrounded with beauty and luxury on every side, and was treated as a loved and honored guest.

It was not long before the hateful wig was cast aside, and Fannie's head was covered with a profusion of dark auburn curls, which were indeed a crown of glory that made her face almost beautiful.

Gentle, loving, and beloved by all, she remained in the seminary until she graduated with honor, after which madam offered her the position of head teacher, with a most liberal salary, which she gratefully accepted.

HOW BESS MANAGED TOM

TOM'S sister Nell was a pretty girl, and being a year older than Tom, wanted to show her authority over him.

The boy was rough and awkward, and just at that age when a boy refuses all meddling with "his rights." He would put his hands in his pockets, his chair on Nell's dress, and his feet on the window-sill.

Of course, they often quarreled: "For pity sake, Tom, do take your hands out of your pockets," Nell would say in her most vexing manner.

"What are pockets for? I'd like to know, if not to put one's hands in," and Tom would whistle and march off.

"Tom, I don't believe you v'e combed your hair for a week!"

"Well, what's the use? it would be all roughed up again in less than an hour."

"I do wish, Tom, you would take your great boots off the window-sill!"

"O don't bother me; I'm reading;" Tom would say: and the boots refused to stir an inch,—which of course was very bad of Tom. And so it would go on from morning till night.

But Sister Bess had a different way of managing her big brother. She seemed to understand that coaxing was better than driving. Sometimes when he sat with both hands plunged into his pockets, Bess would nestle down close beside him, with a book or a picture, and almost before he knew it, one hand would be patting her curls, while the other turned the leaves or held the pictures.

If she chanced to see his feet on the window-sill, she would say, "Just try my ottoman, Tom dear, and see how comfortable it is;" and though Tom occasionally growled in a good natured way about its being too low, the boots always came down to its level.

Whenever his hair looked very rough, she would steal behind him and brush it for him herself, in a way that Tom liked so well that it was a temptation to let it go rough, just for the pleasure of having her do it.

Yet for the next three days at least, he would take special pains to keep every hair in its place, simply to please little sister.

As they grew older, Bess, in the same quiet,

loving way, helped him to grow wise and manly.
If she had an interesting book, she always wanted
Tom to enjoy it with her.   If she was going to call
on any of her young friends, Tom was always invited to go with her.

"I can't understand," said Sister Nell, "why you
should always want that boy at your elbow; he's
rough and awkward as a bear."

"Some bears are as gentle as kittens," declared
Bess, slipping her arm through his with a loving
hug, while "the bear" felt a warm glow at his
heart as he walked away with Bess, and determined
to be "gentle as a kitten" for her sake.

A LITTLE GIRL'S THOUGHTS

WHY does the wind lie down at night
  When all the sky is red,
Why does the moon begin to shine
  When I am put to bed,
And all the little stars come out
  And twinkle overhead?

I see the sun shine all the day,
I gather daisies in my play,
But oh, I truly wish that I
Could see the stars bloom in the sky!
I'd love to see the moon shine down
And silver all the roofs in town,
But always off to sleep I go
Just as the sun is getting low.
             ALICE VAN LEER CARRICK.

Gracie's Disorderly Room

CARELESS GRACIE'S LESSON

GRACIE and Norma Wilson were sisters, aged respectively, fourteen and twelve. But I think that two sisters were never more unlike than were Gracie and Norma. Norma, who was the younger, was as orderly a little lady as one could wish to see, while Gracie was just the reverse.

Often their mother would say, in a despairing tone, "Gracie, I do wish you would care for your room and frocks as Norma cares for hers. Why, you go out with buttons loose, or entirely off your dress, or your frocks unmended, not to speak of the untidiness of your room. If only you would take an interest in such things it would gratify me so much. Without an orderly mind no girl can aspire to become a useful member of society."

Then Gracie would try to make excuses for her shortcomings, pleading this thing or that as the real cause of her negligence. But her poor mother,

at her wits' end to devise some way by which
Gracie might be aroused to a sense of her duty,
would shake her head and say: "Dearest child,
there is no excuse for your slighting your work,
either on your clothes or in your room. You have
plenty of time for both and should force yourself to
perform your share of the labor that falls to you
to do."

And while Mrs. Wilson was thus advising and
entreating her eldest daughter to do her duty in
such small household matters, Norma was busy
tidying up her dainty room or sewing on her summer frocks, mending lace, ribbons, or putting on
buttons and hooks and eyes. She was such a cheerfully busy little miss that Gracie's laziness was the
more pronounced by contrast with her industry.

———

One afternoon, while Gracie was sitting idly
in the hammock which swung in the broad, awn-
ing-covered porch, the phone bell rang and Norma
answered it. The message which reached her ear
made her smile very happily, and she answered,
"Oh, yes, indeed, we shall be delighted to go, and
thank you for both of us ever and ever so much.
What time shall we be ready—at four o'clock this
afternoon? All right. And we shall prepare some
luncheon? Yes, all right, we'll be most happy to
do so. Good-bye."

Then to the porch ran Norma, crying to Gracie,
excitedly: "Oh, sister, Mrs. Jackson has invited
us—you and me—to go with her and Flora and

Tommy for a long automobile ride. We are to stop
on the beach—down at Blake Island—and have
a picnic supper by moonlight. We'll return home
about nine o'clock. Won't that be splendid? I
know mamma will be so happy to have us go, so I
accepted for both of us. Mamma won't be home
for over an hour. And we are to start at four. It
is now two o'clock. We'll have to be stirring if

"We are invited for a long automobile ride."

we are ready when Mrs. Jackson calls. And she
must not be kept waiting."

"Are we to carry luncheon?" asked Gracie,
lazily, not making any sign of getting out of the
hammock.

"Yes. Mrs. Jackson said we'd carry luncheon.
She said she would take sandwiches, cookies, and
jelly. We can supply something else. Suppose
we have some boiled eggs. And I'll run to our

favorite baker's and get a nice cake—one of those delicious white ones, you know. Won't it be splendid?"

"What shall you wear?" asked Gracie, now bestirring herself a bit.

"My pink lawn, I guess," replied Norma. "But I shall have to hurry, for the eggs must be boiled at once, so as to give them time to get cold and solid in the ice box. Otherwise, they wouldn't be fit for the lunch basket."

And away ran busy Norma to the kitchen to put the eggs to boil.

Within a short time Norma had the eggs nicely boiled and cooling in the ice box while she was getting her frock, shoes, hat, and other accessories to her afternoon attire, laid out all ready to wear.

But Gracie was not quite so energetic. She had left the hammock and gone to her own room to look over her frocks to see which one might be fit to wear. A blue dimity was selected as being in the best wearing condition, but in looking it over she found a rent in the skirt and two buttons gone. "Oh, just my luck," she declared petulantly. "I never have a frock in shape to put right on. I do believe I'll ask mamma—if she has returned—to sew on the buttons and mend the rent. Let me see —the lace is all torn in places on my white lawn. The buttons are off my checked batiste. Yes, this blue dimity will be the best." So taking it in her arms, she went down stairs to the sitting room.

Mrs. Wilson had just returned from making

some calls and was listening to Norma's explanation of the good time in store for Gracie and herself that afternoon and evening. "I knew you would not mind our going mamma," Norma was saying, "so I just accepted at the moment."

"No, indeed, I shall not object," said Mrs. Wilson. "On the other hand, I am delighted that Mrs. Jackson has invited you to go with her and her lovely children. You will have a splendid time, I know. And how about your luncheon? Have you everything ready?"

"I am just going to prepare some eggs this very minute," explained Norma. "And," turning to Gracie, "won't you go after some cake and some fruit, sister?"

Gracie frowned. "I'll not have the time." she complained. "And," appealing to her mother, "mamma, will you be good enough to fix this frock for me to wear? I've got to wash and comb and do ever so many things."

Mrs. Wilson shook her head. "Gracie, you must have your lesson first or last. Now is a very good time for it. You must fix your own frock, my child. I have urged you, time and again, to keep your clothes neatly mended. If you let your things go — well, you must suffer the consequences. And, you must assist Norma in preparing the luncheon. It is not fair that she should have the bulk of the work of preparation to do. You must shoulder your share of it."

Gracie, her face aflame with shame, went upstairs

and began to fix her frock. But hardly had she
begun when her mother's voice called to her:
"You would better go for the cake, daughter, before
sitting down to mend. If by any chance you
should not be ready to go when Mrs. Jackson calls
for you, Norma must not be disappointed and shall
have her basket of luncheon ready."

Gracie began to beg off, but her mother was
firm. "Do as I say, daughter, and start at once to
the baker's for the cake. Stop on the way back
and buy a bag of nice fruit."

Gracie had to obey, but did it reluctantly. She
feared she would not be ready to go when four
o'clock arrived, for there was so much to be done
in preparation. She hurried to the baker's and
got the cake; stopped on the way back home and
bought a bag of fruit. But she saw by the town
clock that it wanted only forty-five minutes till
time to start on their automobile outing.

For a moment she felt very much out of sorts
over the fact that she had been obliged to go after
the cake and fruit, but the longer she thought of it
the clearer became her own fault. Yes, she had
been very indifferent about her work. And if she
missed getting the trip—well, it would be her
lesson.

As soon as Gracie gave the cake and fruit into
Norma's hands she ran up stairs to fix her frock.
Norma was all ready, looking as sweet in her fresh
lawn frock as could be. The basket was prepared
for the luncheon, lined with a soft white napkin.

Into the basket Norma put a dozen nicely prepared
eggs, wrapped about with white paper. Then came
the cake, also appetizingly fixed in dainty fashion;
then the yellow oranges, luscious, pink peaches
and golden yellow pears.

At precisely ten minutes before four Norma was
waiting on the porch. At exactly four Mrs. Jackson's automobile came dashing round the corner,
Flora and Tommy in the rear seat and their mother

The Automobile Ride

in front beside the chauffeur. Room for Norma
and Gracie was in the big back seat beside Flora
and Tommy.

"All ready?" called out Mrs. Jackson.

Just as Norma was about to offer some excuse for
her tardy sister, her mother came upon the porch,
and, after chatting in a cordial manner for a few
moments with Mrs. Jackson, she told Norma to
take her basket and go to the automobile. "It is
Gracie's own fault that she is delayed this way, and
she'll have a lesson to-day that she will profit by.

I am quite sure she'll never miss another picnic through her own idleness."

Then, while Norma was getting into the automobile, Mrs. Wilson spoke in low tones to Mrs. Jackson, explaining why Gracie would not be able to go on the outing that day. Although all expressed regrets that Gracie was to be left behind, they knew it was for the best that she be taught a lesson through disappointment.

As the big auto rolled off down the road toward Blake Island, carrying the happy picnic party, Gracie, with tears in her eyes, stood looking from the window after them. And in her heart she knew that her disappointment was due to her own shortcomings. And she vowed to turn over a new leaf from that day.

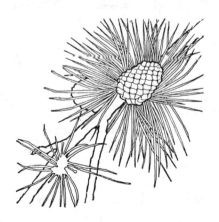

"Are you going to whip Eunice, sir?"

VICARIOUS PUNISHMENT

THIS is the term applied to such punishment as that which Christ bore when he suffered on the cross, the just for the unjust. You do not quite know what it means, do you? I think I hear you say, "Oh, we do not want to know what such long words mean."

But stop a moment, I have a story to tell.

It was a warm summer afternoon; a lazy breeze stole through the windows of a little district schoolhouse, lifting the curtains, and rustling the leaves of the copy-books that lay open on all the desks.

Thirty or forty scholars of all ages were bending over their writing, quiet and busy; the voice of the master, as he passed about among the writers, was the only sound.

Perhaps you might not have thought it possible, but I assure you, that this hot little schoolroom has its heroes and heroines as certainly as many another place which might have seemed far more pretending.

The bell rang for the writing to be laid by; and now came the last exercise of the day, the spelling, in which nearly all the school joined. At the head of the class was a delicate little girl, whose bright eyes and attentive air showed that she prized her place, and meant to keep it.

Presently a word which had passed all the lower end of the class, came to Eunice. The word was *privilege*. "P-r-i-v, priv—i, privi—l-e-g-e, lege, privilege," spelt Eunice. But the teacher, vexed with the mistakes of the other end of the class, misunderstood and passed it. The little girl looked amazed, the bright color came into her cheeks, and she listened eagerly to the next person, who spelt it again as she had done.

"Right," said the teacher; "take your place."

"I spelt it so," whispered Eunice partly to herself; the tears springing to her eyes as she passed down. But too timid to speak to the master, she remained in her place, determining soon to get up again. But her trials were not yet over.

Many expedients had been tried in the school to keep out that arch-enemy of all teachers—whispering. At length the following plan was adopted:—

The first whisperer was stood upon the floor in front of the teacher's desk. Here he acted as a monitor; as soon as he detected another whispering, he took his seat, and the next offender kept a sharp lookout to find some one to take *his* place;

for, at the close of school, the scholar who had the whisperer's place was punished very severely.

This plan appeared to operate very well; every one dreaded to be found last on the floor; but, though it secured an orderly school, many of the parents and scholars doubted its justice.

The boy who was on the floor when Eunice lost her place, was an unruly, surly fellow, who had often before smarted for his faults; and as school drew near its close, he began to tremble. The instant Eunice's whispered complaint reached his ear, his face brightened up; he was safe now. And when the class was dismissed, he said, "Eunice whispered, sir."

Eunice rose, and in a trembling voice related what she had said; but the teacher saw no excuse in it, and she was called to take the place of the ungenerous boy who had told of her.

The books were put away, and the waiting school looked on in sorrow as Eunice left her seat to take the dreaded punishment. She was one of the best scholars; bright, faithful, sweet-tempered, and a general favorite.

Every one felt that it was unjust; and many angry glances were cast at the boy who was mean enough to get a little girl whipped. Overcome with shame and fear, she stood by the side of the desk crying bitterly, while the teacher was preparing to inflict the punishment.

At this moment a tall boy stepped out of his seat, and going to the desk, said :—

"Are you going to whip Eunice, sir?"

"Yes; I never break my rules!" the teacher answered.

"We will not see her whipped!" said the boy in an excited voice; "there is not a boy here but *that* one, who would see her whipped! Whip me, sir, and keep your rule, if you must, but don't touch this little girl!"

The master paused; the school looked on tearfully.

"Do you mean to say you will take her punishment?" asked the teacher.

"I do sir," was the bold reply.

The sobbing little girl was sent to her seat, and without flinching, her friend stood and received the punishment that was to have fallen upon her. The school was dismissed, and the boys paid him in admiration and praise for all he had suffered.

This was vicarious punishment,—one suffering from his own free will the punishment that was to have been borne by another.

You see, do you not, that this is just what He did who bore our sins in His own body upon the tree — the Saviour of men? What He suffered we cannot know in this life; but God laid on Him the iniquity of us all; and this He willingly bore to save us from death. With His stripes we are healed. How great the gratitude each of us owes such a Friend.

> "Love so amazing, so divine,
> Demands my soul, my life, my all."

" I'm awake, mother, come in."

PATTY'S SECRET

MRS. LOMAX softly opened the nursery door and peeped in. "I'm awake, mother," said a voice from the white cot; "come in."

The lady quickly poked the smoldering fire into a blaze and opened the blinds. It was a bitter cold day, and Jack Frost had decorated the windowpanes with silver pictures of forests and castles.

"What wakened you so early, Patty, dear?" asked her mother, coming over to sit on the edge of the bed. To her surprise the young face was wreathed in bright smiles.

"I had such a strange, sweet dream," said Patty, her eyes shining. "I think it must have been my dream that waked me."

"What was it, love?" But Patty was silent. "You don't want to tell me your dream, little daughter?"

"I think I'd rather not, mother, if you don't mind."

"No, I don't mind."

"Well, then, I won't tell it."

Patty's mother had no dream of her own to tell, for she had hardly slept a single one of the many hours between dark and dawn. Many of them she had spent on her knees beside her bed, pouring out her heart in prayer for her darling who was, with the returning day, to undergo a painful and dangerous surgical operation.

For days Patty herself had been in a sad state of nervousness and depression; it had been necessary, for certain reasons, that she should know what was before her, and though she bore up bravely for her years, it could not but be to her like entering a dark cloud.

And yet there was the smile on her lips and the light in her eye, though the hour of trial had come!

The weeks slipped away, each one leaving little Patty stronger than it found her, and nearer to the end of her prison-life behind window panes. For the great trial was safely passed, and the surgeon said one reason that the little girl came so safely through it, without fever or inflammation of any sort, was that she was so quiet and brave, and didn't excite or fret herself.

When Patty heard these praises she only smiled and said, "That's my secret." Though she did not ask, Patty's mother sometimes wondered what she meant and why she would not tell her secret.

But one day Patty overheard a visitor speaking of another child who was to undergo an operation. This visitor was one of the managers of St. Luke's Hospital, and the child she spoke of was a charity patient, a poor, little deformed girl in the public ward. She was an orphan, and had no friends except the kind people at the orphanage where she had been put when only a few months old.

Patty was very quiet until the visitor left; but when her mother turned to her sofa, she found her little daughter eager to tell her something.

"Oh, mother!" she cried, "I must see that little girl; I have something to tell her."

"I'll see her for you, dear," said Mrs. Lomax, "and tell her anything you say."

But Patty, who had been so reasonable and obedient, did not seem able to listen to reason. She wept, and entreated to be carried to the hospital, until at last her mother consented to let her go in a closed carriage with her father to lift her in and out, and carry her every step up and down the halls and stairway. "Only father," she said: "I'd rather have only father."

After all, the drive did not seem to hurt Patty at all; when she had taken off her wraps in the waiting room, and was being carried up to the ward, she whispered a little nervously: "Can I see the little girl all by myself, father?"

Mr. Lomax felt troubled at this almost stubborn secrecy. "I think not, daughter," he said gravely; "the nurse would hardly leave her patient in the hands of such a little girl as you. Why is it that you can't trust me to hear what you have to say?"

Patty hesitated a minute, and then said, "I'm so afraid that you might laugh at it, or say it was just a fancy; and, oh, I could n't stand anybody's laughing, because it helped me so."

"Dear little girl," he said to himself. Then he answered Patty in a very gentle voice: "You need have no fear of that, darling. Now that I know

"Will you ask for me? I don't know Him very well."

how you feel about it, whatever you have to say will be very precious to me."

Nothing more was said, but the little arms tightened about his neck, and he heard a little sigh of content.

Laugh at her! No listener could have smiled at Patty's secret, except as one might smile in glad surprise if an angel spoke.

In very simple speech, as one child uses to another, Patty told this little hospital patient of her long time of suffering and disease; how she had felt that she could not stand the surgeon's table, the knife, the stitches and all the horrors of an operation.

"But the night before it was to happen," said Patty, "after I had prayed with all my might to our Saviour to help me bear the pain I fell asleep, and dreamed that I saw Him.

"Oh, I wish you could know how He looked! Just as if He was all our mothers and fathers in one person. I did not hear Him speak, but I knew from His smile that He was going to be with me. And then I waked up and remembered what He said when He was going back to heaven, 'Lo, I am with you alway,' and I was n't afraid any more after that."

"And did it hurt very much?" eagerly asked the child in the cot.

"I do n't know," said Patty, looking rather puzzled, "maybe it did. The doctor could n't give me as much of the go-to-sleep stuff as he will you; and part of the time I knew what he was doing, and felt the pain. But I did not mind it; I said to myself, 'Why, I can easily stand it; just as long as I must.' You see Jesus had answered my prayer, and He will answer yours, too. Don't forget, what He said about 'Lo, I am with you.'"

"Will you ask for me?" said the little stranger; "I do n't know Him very well."

And Patty promised.

"I do n't believe sugar-sticks are good for little girls."

MOPSEY'S MISTAKE

UNCLE came in one cold evening, looking for all the world like a bear, Louie thought, in his big overcoat. He caught Louie up and gave her a real bear-hug, too.

"Hello, Mopsey! where's Popsey?" he asked.

Popsey was Louie's baby sister, two years old, and her name was n't Popsey any more than Louie's name was Mopsey, but Uncle Jack was all the time calling folks funny names, Louie thought.

"Her's gone to bed," she said.

Then Uncle Jack put his hand in his pocket and made a great rustling with paper for a minute before he pulled out two red-and-white sugar-sticks and gave them to Louie. "It's too bad that Popsey's asleep," said he. But I'm afraid Louie was rather glad of it.

"Are n't you going to save one stick for Grace?" asked mama. Popsey's real name was Grace.

"No," said Louie, speaking low. "I do n't believe sugar-sticks are good for little girls. 'Sides, I want it myself."

Just as she swallowed the last bit there came a little call from her bedroom: "Mama?"

"Hello!" said Uncle Jack, "Popsey's awake!"

And in a minute, out she came in mama's arms, rosy, and smiling, and dimpled.

Then there was another great rustling in Uncle Jack's pocket, and pretty soon —

"This is for Popsey!" said Uncle Jack.

She took her two sugar-sticks in her dimpled hands and looked at them a second — dear little Popsey! — and then she held out the larger one to Louie.

"Dis for 'ou."

"Dis for 'ou," she cooed, "and dis for me!"

Poor Louie! She hung her head and blushed. Somehow she didn't want to look at Uncle Jack or mama. Can you guess why?

"Dis for 'ou!" repeated Popsey, cheerfully, pushing the long sugar-stick into her hand.

"Take it, Louie," said mama.

And Louie took it. But a little afterward mama overheard her tell Popsey: —

"I won't never be such a greedy thing any more, Popsey, dear. And I's always going to divide with you, all the time after this, long's I live!"

"Suddenly, with a great effort, she began to sing."

A GIRL'S SONG

AT the time of the terrible accident a year or two ago at the coal mines near Scranton, Penn., several men were buried for three days, and all efforts to rescue them proved unsuccessful.

The majority of the miners were Germans. They were in a state of intense excitement. Sympathy for the wives and children of the buried men, and despair at their own fruitless efforts, had rendered them almost frantic.

A great mob of ignorant men and women assembled at the mouth of the mine on the evening of the third day, in a condition of high nervous tension which fitted them for any mad act. A sullen murmur arose that it was folly to dig farther—that the men were dead. And this was followed by cries of rage at the rich mine owners.

A hasty word or gesture might have produced an outbreak of fury. Standing near me was a little German girl, perhaps eleven years old. Her pale face and frightened glances from side to side showed that she fully understood the danger of the moment.

Suddenly, with a great effort, she began to sing in a hoarse whisper which could not be heard. Then she gained courage, and her sweet, childish voice rang out in Luther's grand old hymn, familiar to every German from his cradle, "A mighty fortress is out God."

There was silence like death. Then one voice joined the girl's, and presently another and another, until from the whole great multitude rose the solemn cry:—

> With force of arms we nothing can,
>   Full soon are we o'erridden.
> But for us fights the godly Man,
>   Whom God Himself hath bidden.
> Ask ye His name?
>   Christ Jesus is His name.

A great quiet seemed to fall upon their hearts. They resumed their work with fresh zeal, and before morning, the joyful cry came up from the pit that the men were found—alive. Never was a word more in season than that child's hymn.

"Here, that's mine."

CARRIE'S MARKS

FOR I bear in my body the marks of the Lord Jesus,'" repeated Miss Evans, slowly. "My dear girls," she said, "have you these marks? It used to be the custom in India to brand the master's name upon the arms of his servants, so that all who met them would know to whom they belonged. Do your lives show the name of the Lord Jesus to all whom you meet?"

"O Belle!" cried Jennie Day, on the way home. "Did you see Sarah Brooks in that new silk dress? Did n't she feel grand?"

"New!" returned Belle White, "I almost know it was made out of one of her mother's old ones."

"How spiteful they are," thought Carrie Maynard; "I am glad I know better than to talk that way. Girls," she said aloud, "I think you are forgetting very quickly what Miss Evans read about the marks. The Bible says, 'Charity envieth not.'"

"Yes," answered Belle angrily, "and it says, too, 'Vaunteth not itself, is not puffed up.'"

"I wonder if I am conceited, and quote only the verses that do n't mean me," said Carrie to herself. "I am sure humility must be one of the marks;" and she went up stairs and asked God to show her how bad she was, little dreaming how soon the prayer would be answered.

After dinner she washed and wiped the dishes and put them carefully away. "There," thought she, "if 'cleanliness is next to godliness,' I am sure of one mark, for mother says I am an uncommonly neat little girl."

Meantime, Charlie, finding his own library book rather dull, had commenced reading Carrie's. "Here! that's mine," she cried, trying to snatch it.

"Wait till I finish this page," he said, holding it up out of her reach.

"No, I will have it now," she insisted; and by frantic efforts finally seized it, but not till she had left a scratch on his hand, and received several pinches on her arm.

She opened the book, and the first thing she saw was the verse, "Ye have need of patience."

"Oh, dear," she sighed, "there is another mark. Now, I suppose, I must carry this book back to Charlie, and ask his forgiveness."

"I am sorry I behaved so bad, and you may take the book all the afternoon," she whispered.

Charlie stopped whistling. "Upon my word, I believe you are a Christian, Carrie," he said, and then he fell to whistling again. But Carrie went softly up stairs.

" Never mind her! Her father drinks."

SUSIE'S PRAYER

IT was a half holiday. The children were gathered on the green, and a right merry time they were having.

"Come, girls and boys," called out Ned Graham, "let's play hunt the squirrel."

They were all eager for the game, and a large circle was formed with Ned Graham for leader because he was the largest.

"Come, Susie," said one of the boys, to a little girl who stood on one side, and seemed to shrink from joining them.

"Oh, never mind *her!*" said Ned, with a little toss of his head, "she's nobody, anyhow. Her father drinks."

A quick flush crept over the child's pale face as she heard the cruel, thoughtless words.

She was very sensitive, and the arrow had touched her heart in its tenderest place.

Her father *was* a drunkard, she knew, but to be taunted with it before so many was more than she could bear; and with great sobs heaving her bosom, and hot tears filling her eyes, she turned and ran away from the play-ground.

Her mother was sitting by the window when she reached home, and the tearful face of the little girl told that something had happened to disturb her.

"What is the matter, Susie?" she asked, kindly.

"Oh, mother," said Susie, with the tears dropping down her cheeks, as she hid her face in her mother's lap, "Ned Graham said such a cruel thing about me," and here the sobs choked her voice so that she could hardly speak; "He said that I wasn't anybody, and that father drinks."

"My poor little girl," Mrs. Ellet said, very sadly. There were tears in her eyes, too. Such taunts as this were nothing new in that family.

"*He said that father drinks*"

"Oh, mother," Susie said, as she lifted her face, wet with tears, from her mother's lap, "I can't bear to have them say so, and act just as if *I* had done something wicked. I wish father wouldn't drink! Do you suppose he'll ever leave it off?"

"I hope so," Mrs. Ellet answered, as she kissed Susie's face where the tears clung like drops of dew on a rose. "I pray that he may break off the habit, and I can do nothing but pray, and leave the rest to God."

That night Mr. Ellet came home to supper, as usual. He was a hard-working man, and a good neighbor. So everybody said, but he had the habit of intemperance so firmly fixed upon him that everybody thought he would end his days in the drunkard's grave. Susie kissed him when he came through the gate, as she always did, but there was something in her face that went to his heart. A look so sad, and full of touching sorrow for one so young as she!

"What ails my little girl?" he asked as he patted her curly head.

"I can't tell you, father," she answered, slowly.

"Why?" he asked.

"Because it would make you feel bad," Susie replied.

"I guess not," he said, as they walked up to the door together. "What is it, Susie?"

"Oh, father," and Susie burst into tears again as the memory of Ned Graham's words came up freshly in her mind, "I wish you would n't drink any more for the boys and girls do n't like to play with me, 'cause you do."

Mr. Ellet made no reply. But something stirred in his heart that made him ashamed of himself; ashamed that he was the cause of so much sorrow.

After supper he took his hat, and Mrs. Ellet knew only too well where he was going.

At first he had resolved to stay at home that evening, but the force of habit was so strong that he could not resist; so he yielded, promising himself that he would not drink more than once or twice.

Susie had left the table before he finished his supper, and as he passed the great clump of lilacs by the path, on his way to the gate, he heard a voice and stopped to listen to what she was saying.

"Oh, good Jesus, please don't let father drink any more. Make him just as he used to be when I was a baby, and then the boys and girls can't call me a drunkard's child, or say such bad things about me. Please, dear Jesus, for mother's sake and mine."

Susie's Prayer

Susie's father listened to her simple prayer, with a great lump swelling in his throat. When her prayer was ended, he went up to her, knelt down by her side, and put his arm around her.

"God in heaven," he said very solemnly, "I promise to-night, never to touch another drop of liquor as long as I live. Give me strength to keep my pledge, and help me to be a better man."

"Oh, father," Susie cried, her arms about his neck, and her head upon his breast, "I'm *so* glad! I sha'n't care about anything they say to me now, for I know you won't be a drunkard any more."

"God helping me, I will be a *man!*" he answered, as taking Susie by the hand he went back into the house where his wife was sitting with the old patient look of sorrow on her face,—the look that so often rested there.

I cannot tell you of the joy and thanksgiving that went up from that hearthstone that night. I wish I could, but it was too deep a joy which filled the hearts of Susie and her mother to be described.

Was not Susie's prayer answered?

THE STOLEN ORANGE

"MAMMA will never know," thought Flora Marshall to herself, as she took a large orange from the piled-up dish on the table, and, putting it in her pocket, went hastily up stairs.

She was expecting two or three little friends to spend the day with her, and had been busily arranging the doll her kind mother had given her; but while lingering about, waiting for them to come, she was tempted to take one of the oranges which had been placed on the table ready for dinner. She hurried from the room, but had not reached the top of the stairs before her brother's voice stopped her, calling, "Flora, Flora, make haste, I see some of your visitors coming in at the gate;" and directly after there was a knock at the door, and she could hear the voices of Kate and Effie Somers.

Flora ran quickly down stairs, but her face was flushed, and she felt miserable and ashamed as she met her young friends, and took them to the parlor to speak to her mamma.

"Blindman's Buff"

Flora tried to laugh and talk as merrily as any of them, but she could not forget how wrong she had been; and the dish of oranges setting right before her on the table kept her fault ever in her mind. Besides this, not having been able to eat the orange she had taken, she was in constant fear lest she might draw it from her pocket with her handkerchief, and thus be covered with shame in the sight of her young friends.

Poor Flora! she had sinned against God, and against her kind mother, and had spoiled all her afternoon's pleasure for the sake of an orange. At dinner time she could not raise her head to meet her mother's glance, who saw that something was wrong with her, and who said very kindly, "Flora, dear, you are scarcely eating anything—are you not well?" This made Flora ready to cry with shame and repentance. Her conscience was too tender to allow her to be happy while her fault remained unconfessed.

All the afternoon they had merry games, in which everybody joined. They played "Lady's Toilet," "Hunt the Slipper," and many more such games, winding up with "Blindman's Buff." After this the little girls went home, and Flora was left alone with her papa and mama while the younger children were getting ready for bed.

Several times she had fancied she had dropped the orange in some of the rough movements of the games, and had gone more than once quietly into a corner of the room to feel in her pocket if it was still there.   Yes, it was quite safe enough.   "How could I be so wicked and so greedy?" thought Flora ; "mama always gives me as much fruit as is best for me, and yet I have made myself a thief, and after all have not eaten the orange, or been

"Here it is, Mama."

able to put it back, and it has spoiled all my pleasure." She sat still, miserable and unhappy for a little longer, and then her resolution was made—she would tell her mama before she lay down to sleep that night.

With a slow step and a beating heart she went toward the window where her mother was sitting. "Well, Flora," said Mrs. Marshall kindly, "you seem tired and out of spirits to-night; have you come to wish me good-night?"

"O mama!" sobbed Flora, "I have come to tell you how wicked I have been, and how very sorry and miserable I am ;" and hiding her face in the folds of her mama's dress, she told the story.

"Here it is, mama," she said, drawing the orange

from her pocket, "and I think I shall never see an orange again without remembering this bad afternoon."

Very gravely, but gently, her mother spoke to her about her sin, and the consequences it had brought upon her. "I shall not punish you, Flora," she said; "your own conscience has been a sufficient punishment. I have watched your pale, troubled face all the afternoon, and should have wondered what was wrong with you had I not seen you take the orange as I passed the door, which was slightly open. Knowing what you had done, I was not surprised that you seemed unhappy."

"But can you forgive me mama, and believe that I will never do such a thing again?"

"I will forgive you, Flora, because you have told me of your fault; but remember there is One above whose forgiveness you must seek as well as mine, whose eye is always upon you, and who is grieved when you do wrong. Go now, and before you sleep to-night ask God to pardon you, and cleanse you from this and every other sin for the sake of his Son, our Saviour Jesus Christ."

With a sorrowful, repentant heart Flora went to her room, and kneeling there asked God to forgive all her sins, and to help her for the future to resist temptation; but it was a long time before she forgot the stolen orange and how miserable she had been that afternoon.

" He used to chase them and threaten to cut off their ears. "

WEE JANET'S PROBLEM

EVERYTHING small and helpless was once afraid of a certain ragged, barefooted little boy who had recently come to live in the country. His home was the old Perkins' house, in which no one had lived for years; at least no one but wildwood folks, like birds and squirrels. They didn't stay long after the arrival of Pete and his family, because Pete threw stones even at the bluebirds.

Wee Janet was afraid of Pete. All the Primer Class children who attended the country school were afraid of the boy. He used to chase them and threaten to cut off their ears; once he whispered across the aisle to Bessie Saunders that he would like to eat little girls, and she believed it.

The teacher said that Pete was a bad boy. There was never a school day when the child wasn't justly punished for something. It did seem as if no one ever said a kind word about Pete. Wee Janet thought that even his mother was discouraged, because he cruelly teased his own brothers and sisters until they were in tears half the time.

No one in the country knew where Pete and his family lived before they came to the Perkins' farm. In reply to that question Pete said "None of yer business!" to the Sabbath school superintendent.

Wee Janet was much troubled about Pete. "He'll be a dreadfully bad man," she said to her mother, "unless someone can make him into a good little boy. The teacher says she can't do it—she's tried. She says it's a problem."

"I'll tell you what to do, little daughter," said Wee Janet's mother. "Try to think Pete is the lovely boy he might have been if he had been born in the Perkins' house, and dear old Grandma Perkins was his own grandmother."

"But—but my thinker isn't strong enough," objected Wee Janet. "Besides, that wouldn't make Pete into a different kind of a boy."

"No," agreed Wee Janet's mother; "but if you could imagine Pete is lovely, you must treat him in a different way, and it might make him better."

The following day Wee Janet tried her best to do as her mother suggested. The day after she begged all the little girls in the Primer Class to treat Pete as if he were a good boy. At last Wee Janet and the Primer Class gave it up.

"He just gets worse and worse," Wee Janet told her mother. "He says he 'don't care for nuthin' nor nobody,'—that's just what he said."

"Well," replied Janet's mother, "there is one thing you can do, and that is, always be polite and kind to him. 'Overcome evil with good.'"

Days passed. Every night when she said her prayers Wee Janet remembered Pete. Each day she tried to be kind to him in every way known to a little girl eight years old and extremely small for her age. He threw the flowers she gave him into the dusty road and danced on them. He accepted her gifts only to destroy them, every one, and then called her "Cry-baby."

At last the Sabbath-school superintendent learned that Pete was born and had lived all his life in a tenement house in a great city. His father died in State's Prison. After that it seemed to Wee Janet that there was almost no hope for Pete.

One Thursday morning the little girl's mother asked her to carry a pail of buttermilk to Aunt Nancy. "You needn't be afraid to go by the Perkins' house this morning," she said, "because your father was told that Pete went fishing to-day."

Wee Janet was half way to Aunt Nancy's when not far up the road she beheld Mr. Mason's red cow eating grass outside instead of inside the fence.

"Oh, the hooking cow!" exclaimed the child, almost dropping her pail of buttermilk.

At that moment the red cow lifted her head. It is possible she thought that Janet was a big clover blossom. Anyway, on came the cow lowing gently. Mr. Mason always said the cow was harmless.

Janet, too frightened to stir, screamed in terror. That scream brought a barefooted boy running over the fields. That boy was Pete.

"What's the matter, Weejan?" he called.

At that moment Pete looked beautiful to Wee
Janet. It seemed to her that she never saw a finer
looking boy than Pete, the ragged, when he picked
up a stick and made the cow turn around and go
the other way.

"Janet screamed in terror."

"Come on, Weejan," called Pete. "I won't let
her hurt yez. I'll drive her back in her pasture
and lock the gate. Yez see if I do n't!"

After the cow was in her pasture Pete insisted
upon going to Aunt Nancy's with Wee Janet. "Yer
might see a rattler," he explained, as if such a thing
were probable.

"Now I'll take yer home," the boy observed when
Wee Janet found him waiting at the gate. "Yer
too little to be out alone."

Janet's mother thanked Pete for taking care of
her small daughter. Then she gave him a piece of
gingerbread. After that she showed him Wee
Janet's robin's nest and told him all about how the
mother robin worked to build the nest, and how

long she sat upon the eggs before the little nest-
lings were hatched.   Father Robin scolded the
boy so vigorously Wee Janet was afraid Pete's feelings might be hurt.   "You see," she explained, "he
knows that you're a stranger.   Now, Father Robin,

don't make such a fuss.
If Pete took care of me,
he'd take care of your
babies, too.   Would n't
you, Pete.

"Sure!" Pete replied
with a broad grin.

From that hour there
was a change in Pete.
He told Wee Janet's
mother that he never
knew anything about
birds before ; where-
upon he was invited to
come every day to visit
all of Wee Janet's birds'
nests and to read her
bird books.

The Robin's Nest

Before the end of the
year even the little girls in the Primer Class forgot,
or appeared to forget, that Pete was ever a bad
boy.   He is in high school now, in town, and his
mother never looks discouraged when she speaks
of her eldest son, Peter.

As for Wee Janet, to this day she sometimes
wonders how it all came about.

BERTHA'S GRANDMOTHER

BERTHA GILBERT was fourteen years of age, and had just come home from boarding school, where she had finished her first year—a very nice, pleasant school, of about thirty girls, besides the day-scholars; and Mrs. Howard made it, as she promised, a kind of social family, giving each one her personal attention and care. Bertha had improved a great deal in her studies and deportment, and was a very lady-like, agreeable girl.

But as no little boys and girls are perfect, or large ones either, for that matter, I am going to tell you what a mistake Bertha made, and how she was cured of a feeling that might have settled into a very disagreeable habit. Indeed, I have met some grown people who have fallen into the way of treating elderly members of the family with a disregard that bordered on contempt.

Bertha was delighted to be at home once more, to be clasped to her dear mother's heart, to find her father quite improved in health, and her two little

*"**There** was one handsome house which Bertha had often admired."*

brothers as merry as ever; and to meet her dear old grandmother, an old lady who was nearly eighty years of age, yet bright and active, with a fair, sweet face, and silvery hair, which was nearly all covered with a fine muslin cap, the border being crimped in the daintiest fashion you ever saw.

I used to think she looked just like a picture, of a summer afternoon, when she put on a fresh cap and kerchief,—as she used to call the white half square of lawn that she wore round her shoulders, —and her clean, checked apron. In spite of her years, she did a great deal of work around the house, and I do not believe George and Willie would have known how to live without her.

The Gilberts were in very moderate circumstances, for Mr. Gilbert had been compelled to leave his business and retire to the country on account of ill health. This little village of Hillside was a very pretty place. A river ran on one side, and on the opposite side ran a railroad that led directly to New York. Consequently a great many rich and fashionable people lived here, as well as a poorer class.

There was one handsome house which Bertha had often admired. It was the home of very wealthy people—Mr. and Mrs. Bell. The lawn and gardens were very beautiful, and they had an elegant greenhouse and a grapery, indeed, everything that heart could wish. Then Mrs. Bell had traveled nearly all over Europe, and had visited China.

Bertha had met two of Mrs. Bell's nieces at

school; one was a young lady, and the other a little girl not quite as old as herself; but somehow
she and Ada Wilson became great friends. The
two girls were to visit Mrs. Bell during their vacation, and Ada had promised to spend a day with
Bertha—indeed, to come to see her often.

"For Aunt Bell is such a great lady," Ada had
said, "and there are no children; so I'm afraid I
shall be lonesome; and you must return my calls."

The idea of going to the grand house quite elated
Bertha. She told it over to her mother with a
great deal of pleasure.

But nothing ever happens just as one wants it.
The Gilberts' parlor had been repapered, and there
was some delay in getting down the new carpet.
They would surely be in order by the time the
Wilsons arrived, Bertha thought to herself one
afternoon, as she brought her tiny workbasket
to the sitting room and took out a piece of braiding
to finish.

There was a long piazza across the front of the
house. In the center was the hall door—the parlor
being on one side, the sitting room on the other.
As Bertha's eyes roved idly out of the window, she
saw Mrs. Bell's beautiful grays coming down the
road, and a carriage full of ladies. Why, they were
actually stopping; the man handed out two ladies
and a little girl, and opened the gate for them.

Indeed, the Wilsons had reached Hillside a week
earlier than they had expected. When Ada spoke
of her friend, Mrs. Bell proposed that they should

call as early as possible, so that Ada and Bertha might see the more of each other.

"O, mother!" Bertha exclaimed, in astonish-

"O mother! here they are,"

ment, "here they are—Ada and Miss Frances, and their aunt."

"Go and receive them, my dear," said her mother rising.

Mrs. Bell was very gracious, and with a certain unassuming sweetness that immediately set at ease every one with whom she met. She and Mrs. Gilbert exchanged very pleasant greetings. Then they were all led into the sitting room, and Bertha flushed a little. She seemed to see all its shabbiness at a glance—the worn spot of carpet by her father's desk, and another in front of the sofa, the old-fashioned furniture, and grandmother sitting there in her corner, knitting a blue yarn stocking.

Grandma Gilbert rose and courtesied to the ladies. Her dress had no fashionable trail, but showed her low prunella shoes and white, home-knit stockings. She was a prim little body, looking as neat as a pin, but very old-fashioned.

Mrs. Bell presently crossed over to her. "It looks quite like old times to see any one knitting," she said, in her low, pleasant voice. "I think there ought to be a grandmother in every house; they always give a place such a comfortable, home-like look. I remember how my great-grandmother used to knit when I was a little girl."

"It looks quite like old times to see anyone knitting."

"It isn't of much account," returned grandmother. "Stockings are so cheap nowadays; but I do think hum-knit wears better for boys. Willie and George do scour out stockings 'mazin' fast. And then it serves to keep an old woman like me busy."

Ada Wilson glanced up with a peculiar look, and Bertha flushed. The young ladies at Mrs. Howard's were taught to pronounce their words correctly, and were not allowed to use any careless phrases.

Mrs. Bell continued the conversation, however, and grandmother did her best to be entertaining. But she was old-fashioned, and confused her grammar in various ways. Ada, in the meantime, showed a strong disposition to laugh, and finally begged Bertha to take her out to look at the flowers.

"O dear!" she exclaimed, as they went around the walk at the side of the house; "O dear! Isn't your grandmother a funny old woman! I couldn't keep my face sober." Ada laughed as if she considered it very amusing.

Bertha ought to have understood that this was very ill-bred, and espoused her grandmother's cause at once; but instead of that she was ashamed of her, and felt like crying. If she could only have taken her guests

"Isn't your grandmother a funny old woman?"

into the parlor, where they would not have seen grandma!

"Such a funny old woman, with that immense check apron! Bertha, she looks like some of the little old lady pincushions that I've seen, and she makes such a queer mouth when she talks. She hasn't a tooth in her head, has she? and I guess they didn't teach grammar when she went to school. Why do you let her wear that white cap? all the old ladies that I know wear black lace caps, with ribbons. I thought I should laugh outright when she made that little dip of curtsy."

"But she is real old," said Bertha, deprecatingly, "and she has lived in the country most of her life."

"I should think she had come from the back-woods! I wonder she does n't make you wear 'hum-knit' stockings; or do n't you 'scour yours out?' O dear!"

"It is not right to laugh at old persons," Bertha said, summoning all her courage; yet she was mortified and humiliated in the extreme.

"Oh! I do n't mean anything, you know — only it's so funny! You ought to see *my* grandmother. She is nearly eighty, I believe, but she only owns to seventy."

Bertha was too deeply hurt to make any comment. Then Ada kissed her and coaxed her into good humor, telling her of the enjoyments Aunt Bell had in preparation.

When they returned to the room, Mrs. Bell was preparing to leave, and the carriage stood at the gate.

"We have decided on Thursday, Ada," Mrs. Bell said to her niece; "and, Miss Bertha, I have coaxed your grandmother to pay *me* a visit. I think a pleasant old lady, in possession of all her faculties, is rare good company — quite a treat for me. Now, Mrs. Gilbert, I shall send the carriage, and you will be sure not to disappoint me, if you are well."

"You are very kind, indeed;" and grandmother gave another little "dip of a curtsy."

Bertha looked amazed.

She was very quiet after her visitors had gone. Her mother appeared to admire Miss Frances Wilson, and grandma said of Mrs. Bell: "She's a tender, true-hearted Christian lady."

"Mother," said Bertha, the next day, when they were alone; "could n't you fix grandma up a little to go to Mrs. Bell's?"

"Why, she has a nice brown silk dress to wear, and a clean cap and kerchief."

"But she looks so—so—old-fashioned, mother."

"My dear, she is an old-fashioned lady. I think she looks a great deal prettier than to be dressed like people thirty or forty years younger than she is."

"But—"

"O Bertha! you are not ashamed of dear old grandmother?" and Mrs. Gilbert looked at

"I am disappointed."

her daughter in amazement. Bertha's cheeks flushed, and tears came to her eyes.

"My little daughter, I am deeply pained!"

Some way the story came out, and Bertha sobbed away her mortified feeling.

"My dear Bertha!" her mother said, "I am disappointed to see you show so little true courage

Grandma's Early Home in the Wilderness.

and warmth of heart. Ada Wilson has certainly shown herself very ill-bred and heartless in thus criticising so old a person to one of her own relatives. I am not sure but it would be better to decline the invitation altogether."

"O mother! I do not think Ada meant any real harm. She laughs at the girls, and mimics everybody; but she's real good and generous, for all that. And grandma does make mistakes."

"But even if she does, Bertha, when you are tempted to despise your dear old grandmother, I want you to think of her life. When she was a little girl, twelve years old, she went to work in a mill, to help her mother take care of her younger brothers and sisters, and then afterward she took the whole charge of the family upon herself.

"Fifty-three years ago she married a plain farmer, and went West, into what was a wilderness at that time. In her turn, she was left a widow, with a large family, and I shall always honor her for the wisdom she displayed. It would be hard to find four better men than your uncles and papa.

"Aunt Bessy was poor and had a great deal of trouble, but grandma staid with her to the very last, and now she has come to me. I really do n't know what I should do without her, and her life has been most praiseworthy in every respect. She would give her life for any of us. Suppose she were cross and fretful, and thought, as some old ladies do, that we ought to work every moment, and never take a bit of pleasant recreation.

"Instead of this, she is a genial, tender-hearted woman, serving God and doing good every day of her life, and I am sure Mrs. Bell honors her.

"Suppose, Bertha, that I began to fret at her old-fashioned ways, the caps she loves to wear, and the manner in which she expresses herself? It would make her nervous and timid, and if she thought we were growing ashamed of her, I really believe her heart would break. Would you be willing to give her such a wound?"

"Oh, no," returned Bertha, sobbing. "Dear grandmother."

"I think the commandment to honor one's father

and mother takes in one's grandparents equally. And, most of all, I want to see my little daughter brave enough to respect true worth, even if it is not clad in fashionable garments, and fresh from school."

Bertha began to think she had been very weak and foolish, and after a long talk with her mother,

The Carriage Came for Grandma.

she resolved that Ada should never speak so disrespectfully in her presence again.

And so, when Mrs. Bell's carriage came, they started on their visit, grandma looking as fresh and sweet as a rose. In spite of the fact that she was wrinkled, her skin was white and clear, and her soft brown eyes were overflowing with love.

Mrs. Bell welcomed them warmly; but she took possession of grandma, while the young folks amused themselves.

Such a lovely home as it was; full of curiosities, beautiful pictures, handsome statues and elegant furniture!

Some unexpected visitors came in the afternoon,

and Bertha found her grandma quite the center of attraction. She overheard one lady say: "What a charming old lady! I feel like envying her relatives."

As for Ada, she made no further remarks. Her sister had been shocked at her thoughtless levity, and had threatened to inform Aunt Bell, of whom she stood in awe; and so Bertha had a very pleasant visit.

She grew up with a sense of respect for old age; and Bertha Gilbert's pretty manners were often remarked upon. If she met with people less refined than herself, or poorly educated, instead of ridiculing them, she tried to think of their hard lives and few advantages, and was most tender and gracious.

Let us all try to be kind to the poor and aged, for some of them are God's choicest jewels.

PUTTING OFF TILL TO-MORROW

"WHAT made you stop right in the middle of your sentence, and then start talking about something entirely different?" The questioner laughed, and her friend joined as she replied to the puzzled query.

"If I think in time, I make it a rule never to say to-day the mean thing that can be put off until to-morrow," she explained. "So to-morrow it is out of date, and does not get said at all."

NOTHING FINISHED

I ONCE had the curiosity to look into a little girl's work-box. And what do you suppose I found?

Well, in the first place, I found a bead-purse, about half done; there was, however, no prospect of finishing it, for the needles were out, and the silk upon the spools all tangled and drawn into a complete wisp.

Laying this aside, I took up a piece of perforated paper, upon which was wrought one lid of a Bible, and beneath it the words, "I love"—but what she loved was left for me to imagine.

Beneath the Bible lid I found a stocking, evidently intended for some baby foot; but it had come to a stand just upon the little heel, and there it seemed doomed to remain.

Near to the stocking was a needle-book, one cover of which was neatly made, and upon the other, partly finished, was marked, "To my dear—."

I need not, however, tell you all that I found there; but this much I can say, that during my travels through that workbox, I found not a single article complete ; and silent and dumo as they were, these half-finished, forsaken things told me a sad story about that little girl.

They told me that, with a heart full of generous affection, with a head full of useful and pretty projects, all of which she had both the means and the skill to carry into effect, she was still a useless child,—always doing but never accomplishing her work. It was not a lack of industry, but a lack of perseverance.

Remember, my dear little friends, that it matters but little what great thing we undertake. Our glory is not in that, but in what we accomplish. Nobody in the world cares for what we *mean* to do ; but people will open their eyes to see what men and women and little children *have* done.

WHAT'S THE USE

"How much did you ever make by complaining?" asked a man of his "disgruntled" granddaughter. "Come, now, be honest with yourself, and think it all out and see if you do not lose by grumbling."

Finding fault is indeed an unprofitable occupation. It "snarls you up inside," as the little boy said of his hot temper, and so puts you out of joint with the world that you are sure to find something more to grumble about, and so it goes from bad to worse all the while.

"Get away!"

SUSY DILLER'S CHRISTMAS FEAST

PLEAS'M, only a penny. I'm most froze and starved!"

The carriage stood at the edge of the sidewalk, and Mrs. Linley was just going out with her two children to buy some Christmas gifts. Nellie was all scarlet and ermine, her sweet, happy face framed in with golden curls, and Master Frank not a whit behind in elegance, though a trifle more haughty, as you could tell by the wide distance he gave the miserable little beggar.

"Get away!" said Mrs. Linley, with a disdainful sweep of the hand.

The woman and the child looked at each other—one of those glances that stamp a face upon one's memory. Mrs. Linley was always afraid of street trash. They might have fever, or small pox, or some other infection, lurking in their rags.

The carriage drove on. The children were happy, generous, well-behaved, and belonged to a Christian family. They were going to prove all this now. Besides gifts for mama and papa, and some little cousins, half a dozen poor children were to be remembered.

They spent all the pleasant, sunshiny middle of the day going from shop to shop. What hosts of tempting things! A perfect Santa Clause revel everywhere. It was like a glimpse of fairy-land.

Frank and Nellie laughed and talked, ran to mama with a hundred pretty things, but did not tease.

They had quite a load in the carriage. And oh! wouldn't lame Johnny Ashton be delighted with his books, and the wheel-chair mama had bought him, and Susy Dorr would be the happiest of the happy in her new plaid dress, and her teacups and saucers.

"Poor children love to play just as well as rich children, don't they, mama?" said grave, sweet Nellie.

"I hope you will never forget, my dear, that we are all created alike, and that all the poor little ones are just as precious in God's sight."

"And it is so nice to make them happy!"

Mrs. Linley gave her darling a smile.

"And Christ the Lord was born for everybody," Frank added in a reflective manner. "My teacher told me so on Sabbath,—so that all little children might be saved, and,—have a merry Christmas."

"Maybe they can't all have a merry Christmas. Some are very poor and sick, and nobody seems to care for them—like the little beggar-girl who stood watching us when we started. O mama! isn't it hard? What becomes of them?"

The sweet face was full of tender pity.

"God takes care of them, like the sparrows," said Frank.

Mrs. Linley did not answer. Already her heart condemned

"They shivered with the cold."

her, for after all, she was a kind-hearted woman. She half expected to find the wretched object on her doorstep. If so, she would try to make amends for her harsh words. But she was not there.

When they returned home from shopping, they shivered with the cold and ran to the register. Then papa came home, and they had the happiest Christmas eve imaginable. Of course one cannot make one's charities go all around the world, but Mrs. Linley thought she had stretched hers a long distance. So she had. And yet she might have given the child at her door a few pennies. But street-beggars were so often thieves!

Meanwhile the little beggar girl wandered on. For nearly a week she had slept in the station-house and begged a little during the day, just enough to keep body and soul together. She used to sell matches and pins, but she had no capital to buy a new stock, and there were so many in the trade. A month ago the old woman with whom she had lived died suddenly. Then she had to live the best she could.

She went on asking now and then for a penny. Some gave the forlorn little beggar a scowl, some did not even deign to look, and one or two men spoke roughly to her. Oh! She was so hungry and so cold.

The bright sunshine did not seem to warm her a bit. She looked wistfully into basement windows. She stared at the merry, happy children who ran by in warm clothing. Her shoes were out

"She came to a restaurant"

to the ground; her tatters flapped in the biting wind.

It was growing colder and colder. She ran along until she came to a restaurant. Such a delightful, savory smell came through the grating, and a faint warmth that was most grateful to her. Not a mouthful of anything had she eaten since yesterday noon. People went along with great market baskets full; men with bundles in their arms, girls and boys with Christmas gifts,—all hurrying homeward.

"Move on, move on, there!" said the stern voice of a policeman.

What if she was arrested and sent to prison? She would have something to eat. And the pain gnawing at her stomach was so hard to bear. There was a jacket she might steal—the men around would be sure to see her. She reached out her hand.

No, she couldn't. She never had been a thief. She remembered her mother, who had died two years ago. The pretty lady getting into the carriage had made her think of *her!* Oh! how good it was that the dear mother could never be hungry again. And she had said, "Jennie, *never tell a lie, never steal.*"

She sat down on a doorstep and began to cry. It was very cold now, and she was so chilled that the tears froze on her thin cheeks. She curled herself up in the corner. If she could only get to sleep.

"Hillo!" said a cheerful voice, and some one

shook her by the shoulder. "You'll freeze to death here! It's pinching cold! You better run home."

"Lemme be. I haven't any home. And I was almost asleep. You've brought all the old pain back."

Sturdy young Susy Diller, herself a poor working girl, dragged up the forlorn little object and scanned the thin, blue face.

"Where have you been?"

"Station-houses and such," the child answered sullenly. "After old Molly died, they turned me out. I hadn't any capital, so I had to go out of trade. I've tried to beg —"

Susy stood considering. What would Granny say if she brought the poor thing home? "Don't you ask another one to your Christmas party," she had said already. "There won't be room for 'em to stand on

"She sat down on a doorstep and began to cry."

one foot." Susy drew her sleeve across her eyes. Somehow her heart had grown very tender since she had been going to the mission school. A little scene flashed into her mind: On Sabbath, Mr. Linley, the most splendid man in the world, Susy insisted to Granny, had been explaining to the boys and girls how even the Saviour of all the world had been houseless.

"I wish I'd been there!" said Susy bravely, "I'd a' took Him in."

"Susy," replied Mr. Linley, "when we do such a thing for the very poorest and meanest, we do it for the Lord." And then he read the beautiful commendation that the Saviour was to bestow at the last upon those who did what they could in this world, picturing their blessed joy and surprise as they said: "Lord, when saw we Thee hungry and fed Thee, or sick and ministered unto Thee?" He had a way of making such vivid pictures that the boys used to listen wide-eyed and open-mouthed.

So Susy had announced to Granny that she meant to give a Christmas party, and repeated to her all the conversation at the Sabbath-school as she always did.

"I thought you was going to get that nice new jacket? And you have just money enough."

"I'll wait two or three weeks for that," declared Susy. "You see it's so much nicer on Christmas. I don't understand a bit how the Saviour did come down to earth, but it seems good to think He was a little boy, though He was a good sight better'n any of us. When you think of all that, you can get kinder nigh to him, just as I do to Mr. Linley, our Sabbath-school teacher.

"And maybe, if we ask in the poor and lame, He will look down and think Susy Diller is trying to keep Christmas the right way. There'll be lame Tim Jenkins,— you know he was run over by the street cars,— and Humpy, whose mother is dead, and the little Smith that I set up in the paper business, and Kit Benner, who's been sick and lost his place, and —"

It was then that Granny had said: "Do n't ask another one. There won't be room enough for 'em to stand on one foot."

"And we'll have a rousin' turkey,—I know where I can get one real cheap,— and cranberry sauce, and pickles, and mince pie. A regular feast, and no mistake!"

But finally Susy had found two more; so now there were six of them. Susy had work in a factory and took care of Granny, who was too old to do much of anything, and was almost bent double with rheumatism. They had a room on the second floor of a tumble-down barrack, and one small bedroom out of it; but Granny thought it almost a palace, because Susy was so good to her.

And now here was one more to share their Christmas dinner. What would Granny say! But the young missionary did not stop long to consider the matter,— here was a case of real suffering, and Susy's conscience quickly adjusted itself · —

"Come along," said Susy to the little vagrant, thinking somehow of the Lord of all who had not where to lay His head.

"For maybe if He was here," she soliloquized, "we should n't be able to tell Him from anyone else.   And it's just—anybody."

Susy took the little estray by the arm, and hurried her along.   Poor little Jennie! her feet seemed

"She dropped into a little heap before the fire."

hardly to touch the ground, they were so cold and numb.   She did n't much care even if she was being taken to the station house.

But she was n't.   After a while she felt the warmth and heard the voices, but she was so tired and sleepy that she dropped into a little heap before the fire and only heard her young rescuer say : —

"Let her sleep, Granny; it'll do her more good than anything else."

"It was a famous Christmas feast."

"But, Susy, child, we can't take care of her all the time. And—" Granny stopped there, looking into Susy's eyes.

"It's Christmas eve, Granny. I feel as if we ought to do something, even if we have only a manger to take people into."

By and by, Jennie Morgan, the poor little waif, woke up, had some supper, and told her story. It was like hundreds of others, only her mother was a beautiful lady. She had seen some one in the street this morning that looked just like her.

"She's smart and chipper, Granny, and she'll soon be better," said Susy.

Jennie's cheeks were very red the next morning, and her eyes very bright; moreover, her voice had a curious tremble in it, but she declared she was quite well. It was so delightful to be housed and warm, and to have no great hungry pangs gnawing at her stomach.

Susy went out a while, and Granny prepared her turkey to roast. Poor Jennie thought there never had been such a savory fragrance before.

It was a famous Christmas feast. There were lame Tim with a clean face, and a new red necktie to do honor to the occasion; Humpy, as the little fellow was called, who sold pins, tape, and shoe strings on the corner, and had grown deformed from a bad fall; Kit Benner, looking white enough and thin enough to frighten you; three others, and the little stray Jennie Morgan, besides Granny, in a new cap and new calico gown.

Such a time as they had! They were so crowded around the table that they had hardly elbow room. They made jokes, laughed, drank Granny's health in the fragrant coffee, and were as happy as the happiest.

Meanwhile, over at Mr. Linley's they had a grand tree. Nellie, dressed like a fairy, distributed the gifts, carefully laying aside those for the poor. Of course they could not ask such people into their festivities. It was honor enough to hang their gifts on their beautiful tree. Then Mrs. Linley played, and they had some charming carols.

They had two or three songs sung also at Susy Diller's. Susy had learned them at the mission school. Finally Jennie begged to lie down in the corner by the stove, for she felt a little chilly, and her head was aching.

"O Susy, won't you sing again?" she pleaded. "It's like heaven. Mother used to tell me about it. And do you suppose that the Lord Jesus cares for little girls who have to live on the street and sleep where they can? Sometimes they can't help lying and stealing."

"Yes, He *does* care. Mr. Linley told me so. You see," and Susy laid her forefinger in the palm of the other hand, "you see this is the way: He puts the thought into other people's hearts, 'cause He isn't here any more to do the work."

"Oh!" said Jennie slowly, and with a sage nod, " would n't it be good, Susy, if He would put it into the hearts of rich folks? they could do so much."

"Sometimes He does. Look at the newsboys' dinner! And there's a good many things."

Poor Jennie sighed a little. She could not make it out straight in her tired brain.

The crowd went away presently, declaring that it was the jolliest sort of a Christmas. They thanked Susy and Granny over and over again.

The next day was Sabbath. Susy begged Mr. Linley to come and see the little sick girl at her house. And one way and another, the story of the Christmas feast came out.

For Jennie, the little beggar girl, was very sick. Cold and hunger had done their worst. It had been so hard and dreary since her mother died, with no one to care for her, and to have to dodge around continually, kicked and cuffed and almost starved. And if the Lord up above *did* care—

"She's a pretty sick little girl," said Susy, "but Granny and I will do our best to pull her through."

Mr. Linley felt the pulse and shook his head. The fever was high and there was no strength to battle with it.

And then he looked into Susy's great, wistful eyes, and was touched to the heart. The child had learned the sweetest and noblest lesson of all. She had gone out into the highway and hedges, she had gathered in the lame and the halt and the blind.

"You see I've grown fond of her, a'ready," explained Susy. "I'd do anything for her."

"I'm afraid it's too late. I will send in a doctor, and some delicacies from the house."

"If you please, I'd rather not have you do the last. You see Granny spoke a little cross at first, and now she's trying to make it all up to her. She'll feel better if she does everything ; and she's a good heart, has Granny."

What a point of conscience here amid poverty and ignorance!

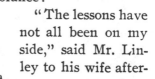

"The lessons have not all been on my side," said Mr. Linley to his wife after-

"O Mother! Mother!"

ward. "The poor little factory girl has taught me something that I shall never forget. To think of her going without her coat that she might provide a dinner for some homeless, hungry children. I wish you would go and see them, my dear." Mrs. Linley went with her husband.

Susy stared as if she had seen an angel. Granny dropped a curtesy, and dusted a chair with her apron.

"Little Jennie," Susy whispered, "poor little girl, can't you open your eyes a minute?"

She opened them — wider — wider. Then she rose a little and stared around — stretched out her trembling hands toward Mrs. Linley, and cried:—

"O mother! mother! Susy said I should find you. I tried to be good, not to lie or steal, though I was nearly starved. And Susy's been so — kind. She brought me in — to the Christmas — dinner — "

Mrs. Linley caught the swaying form in her arms. The last words quivered slowly on her lips and her eyes drooped. She remembered just where she had seen the child, and a pang of bitter self-upbraiding pierced her heart. She kissed the still lips for her mother's sake, and laid her gently down. Had Susy and Granny entertained an angel unawares, while her blind eyes had not been able to discern "the least of these?"

"Oh!" said Susy sobbing, "I'm so glad you came. I s'pose she thought it was her own mother, for she has talked about her all the time. Poor little girl! I shall always be thankful that I brought her in out of the cold, though I never guessed she was going to die."

"The fame of your Christmas feast has gone up among the angels, Susy," said Mr. Linley reverently. "And now, my dear girl, have little Jennie buried where you like, and bring the bill to me. I want a little share in your good work."

Mr. and Mrs. Linley walked home quietly. Had her beautiful Christmas tree borne any such fruit as this?

"For I was an hungered and ye fed me."

THE BARN THAT BLOSSOMED

MOTHER, it was dreadful!" Gerry's face was all shades of soberness, and her voice had a suspicious quiver in it. "I almost wish I hadn't seen. The house is fairly tumbling down; they couldn't have been warm once last winter. And there were five of them, from the baby up to Tad; he's twelve. Such clothes! Just as if somebody's rag-bag had fallen apart and begun to walk around. No wonder poor little Mrs. Jimson is nothing but a mite of discouragement. Old Jim wasn't much of a man; but I suppose he did put a bite inside of the rags once in a while, and she doesn't know where even that is coming from, now he's gone. At least, not bites enough to satisfy five unragged appetites."

Mother Brace's hands fell upon the potato-pan, knife and all. "Why, Gerry, child, what can we do? Our own bites aren't any too big; but I suppose we can spare a few vegetables now and again, if any grow without old Jim to hoe them. But we certainly haven't any houses or extra clothes, unless—maybe I could spare—"

"You can't spare a single clo', you blessed mother!" interrupted Gerry. "You're not to worry at all, but I am going to think and think. I'm sure I shouldn't be made to feel so bad if there wasn't something I could do to help."

With which cheerful logic she sprang up and set about finishing her morning's work, interrupted to attend the short and simple funeral service said over the body of "old Jim Jimson," who had given them such help as they could not dispense with in their square bit of garden, and squandered the money that should have provided for the wife and five children whose wretchedness had torn Gerry's tender heart.

All day she thought and thought; and, as she washed the supper dishes, she was still thinking:—

"Now, Gerry Brace, what are your worldly possessions, anyway? Clothes enough to be a wee bit more than respectable, a house plenty big for two, but certainly not stretchable to take in six more, a little piece of garden, and a nice big piece of grass and trees, and a barn. A barn!" she repeated, clasping her hands in the dish-water with a splash.

"Mother Brace," she said ten minutes later, when she sat on the top step of the front porch with her arms across her mother's knee. "I believe I've hit on the very thing to do. There are the

Jimsons in their tumble-down house, and here are
we with a perfectly whole, clean barn without even a cat in it. Do n't you see the possibilities? Presto! Change! There is the tumble-down house empty, and here are the Jimsons living in the perfectly whole barn."

Mother Brace gasped.

"But Gerry—"

"Oh, mother dear, please do n't 'but.' You know

"I believe I've hit on the very thing to do."

there are two parts to the barn down-stairs, and up-stairs there are three. They could have a living-room, kitchen, and three bed-rooms."

"Yes'm," said Mother Brace meekly, "but where would they get the three beds?"

"Why, I suppose they sleep on something now, though probably it would n't fit our clean barn; that's a fact."

For a moment Gerry looked crestfallen. Then she brightened again.

"Well, I can think that out, too, seeing I thought of the barn. The question is, mother, would you be willing to have them come!"

There was silence on the porch for a few minutes while Mother Brace watched the sunset over beyond the hills.

"It looks like the gates of the celestial city," she said at last, "where there are homes for everybody. Yes, Gerry, dear, I'd be willing to have them come, if there's anyway of fixing it."

Gerry squeezed the work-roughened hand that had slipped into hers.

"You blessed! Of course, I knew you would. Mother, I'm going to Aunt Serinda about the beds."

"Your Aunt Serinda?" Mother Brace gasped again. "Why, Gerry!"

"Yes'm," repeated Gerry. "I'm going to Aunt Serinda. There is no sense in having a garret full of old furniture when there's an empty barn just hungry for it. If she has n't enough, I'll go to

Mrs. Squires. I'll take up a collection, mother, a missionary collection."

"I'm afraid your Aunt Serinda will think—" began Mother Brace faintly.

"Yes, I know she will think," Gerry agreed. "She will say, 'How perfectly ridiculous!' But before I get through she will give me a bed and very likely a blanket. I shall start out to-morrow morning and see what I can do."

True to her word, the sun had not dried the dew from the grass that was rapidly growing green under its spring warmth before Gerry was on her way up the neat box-bordered walk at Aunt Serinda's.

"The Jimsons!" sputtered that good woman when Gerry began to dilate upon their forlorn condition. "Jimson weeds I call 'em. Of all the shiftless, good-for-nothing lots! They can't be much worse off now old Jim's gone."

"No, ma'am," said Gerry; "they don't need to be. They are going to be better off, Aunt Serinda. They're coming to live in our barn. You know we never use it, and it's a specially tight barn, with more windows than most."

Aunt Serinda held up her hands in horror.

"In—your—barn? How perfectly ridiculous! Why, they'll bring microbes enough to poison you all. And they'll run over everything."

"I hope so," said Gerry promptly. "Little Jimson-weeds have to run somewhere. It might better be over our good clean grass than down there in the centre where there's mischief waiting to be done every minute. They won't bring any microbes, though, because I mean to have them burn up all their old things before they come. I'm taking up a collection this morning to furnish the barn. You are going to give me a bed and some other things out of the attic, are n't you, auntie?"

"Well, of all things!" Aunt Serinda stood with her hands on her hips, and stared at Gerry. "If you are'nt the beat of any girl I ever saw! I suppose you'd like to have me take down my kitchen stove for 'em, and send along the spring rocker, from the parlor, besides."

Gerry laughed cheerily.

"Oh, no, auntie, only just the things up in the attic that you can spare as well as not. You know you'd rather someone would have the use of them than to have them wasted up there. Could n't we go up now and see? I ought to hurry a little. I may have to go to lots of places before I get enough."

Aunt Serinda turned, and led the way up stairs without a word.

"There is a bed," she admitted when they stood under the peaked roof. "I took it down from the spare room when Mary Ellen bought the brass one to sleep in when she comes. The mattress would n't fit any other; so I suppose it might as well go along. There's some patchwork quilts in that chest, too, that Mary Ellen never liked. I guess you could have some of those."

"It was very exciting, picking out and setting

aside.   Just why Aunt Serinda, with all her abundance, had treasured so many old things was a question.   Probably it was because few people knew

"It was very exciting, picking out and setting aside."

the keys to her heart as Gerry did, and so no one
had ever asked her for them.   And it was not
Aunt Serinda's nature to give without asking.

Once started, however, it seemed to be easy
enough.

"Those chairs over there," she said finally, dusting her hands upon her apron when the collection
had grown to a very respectable size, "they do n't

need much mending; I guess James can do it to-night. How are you going to get all this stuff over to the barn?"

"I do n't know." Gerry paused aghast. "I never once thought of that. I'll find a way, though, or make it."

"Yes, I expect you would," said Aunt Serinda, smiling grimly; "but this time you need n't. I'll have James hitch up the long wagon and take 'em over when you're ready, and he could pick up anything else you collect, on the way."

Gerry stood for a minute with shining eyes, irresolute. Then she flew at Aunt Serinda, and, throwing both arms around that astonished person's neck, planted a warm kiss on the nearest cheek.

"Auntie, you're a—a winter apple! Just as crisp and reliable and sweet inside! I like you."

"Mercy me!" said Aunt Serinda, quite abashed. "Mercy me!"

The quarter of a mile down the road to Mrs. Squires' house seemed to slide from under Gerry's feet. Mrs. Squires was round and rosy and sympathetic.

"Why, yes, my dear, of course, I'll help. I'm through cleaning, and there are some things I've been wondering what to do with. I have n't any beds, but there is a rusty cook-stove in the cellar that I'll be only too glad to have you take. I should think it could be cleaned up and do very well."

"Oh, yes, thank you," said Gerry eagerly; "I

can black it and all that. And Aunt Serinda's
James will come for it."

There were several additions to the cook-stove
before Gerry hurried on to Judge Beaker's, following the suggestion that the Beaker girls had just
refurnished their bedroom.

It was close after house-cleaning time, and rum-
mage sales had not yet found their way into East
Greenfield; so it was not very wonderful that by
noon Gerry really had enough things promised her
to furnish the barn with a comfort that would
seem luxury to the young Jimsons and their
mother.

It must be confessed that the finishing touch for
Gerry was given when she leaned on the window-
sill to tell the story to little lame Ruthie West, not
because she expected anything there, but because
she was so happy that she could not help stopping
to share it with some one. Ruthie laughed over
the yellow soap feelingly offered by Mr. Evans, and
cried over the cook-stove, and when it was all told
exclaimed earnestly : —

"Oh, Gerry, I must do something ; I just must!
I haven't any things, even if you needed them ;
but you come in, please, and get my Japanese box
out of the bureau drawer. It's got my gold piece
in it. It's truly mine, Gerry ; Mr. Graves gave it
to me last Christmas, and I haven't been able to
think of anything nice enough to do with it. Now
I know. You take it, Gerry, and buy some pretty
stuff to make some frilly things, and some curtains,

maybe—if there's enough. They'll love to have pretty things; I know they will. And, Gerry, maybe it will help them to be good, those little Jimson-weeds," quoting Aunt Serinda softly.

Tears rolled down Gerry's cheeks onto the shining piece of gold in Ruthie's hand.

"You—darling!" she whispered, and could not say anything more.

Mother Brace's potatoes grew quite cold while she listened to Gerry's excited reports, and grew as much excited herself in the hearing.

"I'll begin to sweep the barn this afternoon," she declared, hustling the dishes off the table. "I do n't want that poor Jimson soul to wait a minute longer than she must to have it all."

The dust was flying in clouds from the open barn doors when the "poor Jimson soul" herself came dragging up the path with the baby in her arms and a dingy black dress, manifestly borrowed, trailing forlornly behind her.

"Oh, my!" thought Gerry as she watched her coming. "I never remembered the clothes. They'll have to have them. I wonder—

"Come right in, Mrs. Jimson," she interrupted herself; "come and sit down here. You must be tired with such a long walk."

"I ain't no more tired than I always am," Mrs. Jimson answered drearily, dropping into the rocker Gerry pushed forward. "I ain't never been rested, and I do n't never expect to be. I've come to see if you've got anything I can do to earn some money.

Folks has been good, and we've had enough to eat so far; but it stands to reason I've got to do something myself."

"Yes," Gerry nodded gravely, "and the children will have to help. Maybe Tad can do some of the gardening ol — Mr. Jimson used to do, and Jennie's big enough to take care of the little ones and help do the housework so you can go out part of the time."

"I guess all the housework won't hurt her," sighed Mrs. Jimson, brushing away a slow tear that was stealing down her cheek. But at the same moment a ray of hope began to steal into her heart with Gerry's brisk planning.

"I'd be willing to do anything," she went on more energetically. "I ain't lazy, though folks may think so; but I've got plum discouraged."

"And now you are going to take heart o' grace and begin again," declared Mother Brace, coming in with her broom over her shoulder in time to hear the last words. "I suppose, then, you're willing to come and scrub my barn floors for me tomorrow morning. They won't be very hard, but I can't get down so long on account of my knee. I can pay you fifty cents."

"Oh, I'll come." Mrs. Jimson straightened up so eagerly that she nearly dropped the baby. "And I'll get 'em clean, too. I know how if I do n't look it."

Telegraphic signs passed between Mother Brace and Gerry by which it was decided to say nothing about the moving at present. Nevertheless Mrs. Jimson went home much lighter of heart and foot than when she came, though she carried several extra pounds in the way of vegetables and fresh bread.

Hardly was she out of sight when Mrs. Thomas Benton, president of the Ladies' Aid Society, rapped at the Braces' front door.

"You see," she told Gerry when she had recovered her breath, being somewhat portly for so steep a hill, "we've heard about your barn plan, and we thought we'd better have a finger in the pie. So we decided that instead of packing a barrel for the heathen just now we will dress up the Jimson's, so as to have them match better with their new home. Oh, we shall do the heathen before long, too; only we thought maybe this was an 'ought to have done and not leave the other undone.'"

Bright and early next morning Mrs. Jimson was on her knees scrubbing the barn floors, little dreaming that she was helping to lay the foundation for her own future happiness.

She could not have been more thorough, had she known, much to Mother Brace's satisfaction.

"There's good stuff in her," was the verdict. "She may be a weed, but she'll pay for cultivating."

It was nearly a week before the barn was ready, a week so busy that Gerry's bones ached when she stretched them in bed each night, but so happy that she cared not at all for the aches. Aunt Serinda's James toiled up and down the hill with the long wagon loaded more than once; Ruthie's loving fingers flew upon the ruffles and frills; Gerry and her mother set things straight, nailing and tacking diligently; and gradually the barn became transformed.

"It's blossomed like the rose!" Gerry announced joyously. "It isn't a barn any longer; it's a cottage. Oh, mother, it's better than a cottage; it's a home."

Oh, it was very plain and simple; to some it might even have seemed bare, in spite of Ruthie's pretty things. But to Gerry, with the tumble-down house fresh in her memory, it was all that could be desired.

The morning it was all ready at last, in spotless order, with the bright sunshine and the

"Mrs. Jimson was on her knees scrubbing the barn floor."

soft spring breezes pouring in at the open windows,
Gerry ran down the hill to the Centre.

The little Jimsons were not playing in the mud
outside the tumble-down house as usual. Mrs.
Jimson met Gerry at the door in a trim dark calico
dress that made a different woman of her. Seated
in a beaming circle within were the five children,
each clad from top to toe in clean, fresh garments,
from Tad down to the baby, who was crowing in
Jennie's arms, radiant in a gay pink gingham.

"Are'nt we splendid, Miss Gerry?" cried the little girl, pushing a glowing face out from behind
the baby's head. "Ma's just got us dressed up,
and we're going to have a bonfire of the old ones."

"It was the Ladies' Aid, Miss Gerry," supple-
mented Mrs. Jimson almost as excitedly. "They've
just gone, Mrs. Benton has, and they brought us
all these and more. Did you ever see anything
like it? Of course, I'm going to help clean the
church to help make up," she added with a new
womanly dignity that was very becoming; "but I
could n't never pay for the kindness, never!"

"It's beautiful," said Gerry, "beautiful! I
could n't tell how glad I am. I'm so glad, too,
that you've got them on, for mother wants you to
come up to the house a few minutes, all of you.
It's something very important."

Seizing Tommy, the two-year-old, by the hand,
she hurried off ahead of them, fearing she could
not keep her secret if she delayed another instant.
Up the hill and across the wide grassy yard she

"We want to show you our new house."

led them, straight to where Mother Brace stood in the barn doorway.

"I've brought them," she said, and stopped, overwhelmed by this crowning moment.

"We want you to see our new house we've fixed up," Mother Brace explained, coming to the rescue. "Come in, all of you."

Considerably bewildered, Mrs. Jimson obeyed, shooing the children before her like a flock of chickens. It was not usual for her to be called upon for opinion or approval; and she made the most of it, exclaiming with admiration and delight as they made the rounds of the tiny bedrooms, and stood once more in the long, shining kitchen with its neatly blackened stove and its row of polished tin pans.

"It could n't be no completer, no ways," she pronounced judgment. "Nor no prettier."

Then Gerry found her voice, and the words came tumbling out in joyful haste.

"It's all for you, Mrs. Jimson. You're to come here this very day, and this is to be your home. You are to sleep in the bedrooms, and cook in the kitchen, and —"

"But I do n't understand," faltered Mrs. Jimson, her bewilderment deepening with every second. "Where did it come from? Whose is it? How —"

"It came from everybody," laughed Gerry tremulously. "Lots of people helped. And it's yours, I tell you, to live in as long as you want to, you and the children. Do n't you see, dear?"

Little Mrs. Jimson dropped down suddenly in the middle of the shining floor.

"Oh, my land! my land!" she sobbed, rocking to and fro. "I never knew there was such folks in the world. I feel just as if I'd got into one o' the many mansions!"

Mother Brace patted the bent shoulders gently.

"You have," she said, her voice catching, "into one He's been preparing for you. Only instead of angels He used a lot of warm, loving human hands to do it with."

"I SHALL NOT WANT"

"The Lord is my shepherd, I shall not want."

I shall not want food. "I am the bread of life. He that cometh to Me shall never hunger."

I shall not want drink. "If any man thirsteth let him come unto me and drink."

I shall not want rest. "Come unto Me all ye that labor and are heavy laden, and I will give you rest."

I shall not want guidance. "I am the way; no man cometh unto the Father but by Me."

I shall not want companionship. "I have called you friends." "Lo, I am with you always."

I shall not want joy. "These things have I spoken unto you that My joy might remain in you, and that your joy might be full."

I shall not want honor. "If any man serve me, him will My Father honor."

"We shall find plenty to do to-day."

HOW DOROTHY HELPED THE ANGEL

TWO angels met one misty morning in one of the Lanes of Light: one, the Angel of Encouragement; the other, the Angel of the Rainbow, who brightens things up generally.

"We shall find plenty to do to-day, companion," remarked the latter; "things are looking rather gloomy."

"Ah!" said the Angel of Encouragement, "how blessed are we who carry heaven's sunlight ever with us, and ever round us!"

And then they parted.

The Angel of Encouragement entered a house where a young girl was trying to light a fire. A gray, weary day stretched in front of her, and the tears would come. Some girls of her age were still at school. She was a girl with ambitions; many a rosy castle of fancy had been built by her, but built only to vanish.

The angel bent over her, and whispered: "Try to encourage somebody to-day." And thinking it

"Encourage somebody."

was her own inner self that had spoken, she answered, "Yes, perhaps that is the wise way after all."

Directly breakfast was over a postcard had to be taken to the letter box for mother. The angel's thought had brought a bright light into the girl's face. A little fellow was coming towards her, and he was cry-ing; the school bell had awakened fears. Instantly her arm was round his neck.

"Cheer up! It will soon be going-home time."

"Will it?" asked the child, and his sobs ceased.

"Yes. I felt like crying this morning. But it's better to be brave."

A business man was hurrying along, but paused to watch the work of comforting. His heart was heavy, too, but her words:

"Cheer up."

"It will soon be going-home time—it's better to be brave," like a sweet chime, kept with him all the day.

As the girl re-entered the house a song was on her lips, and a tired woman turning a washing-machine next door caught it. She looked round

her—there was such a heap of work to do—and
dinner to think of for husband and children.   No
wonder there was a worried look
on her face.

"Hope on! hope on!
  Though long the road and drear.
Hope on! hope on!
  The sunlit hours are near."

It was Dorothy Cummins singing! "Hope on!"   The woman
began to sing too.   "The sunlit
hours are near!"   The washer

"Hope on."

went faster.   The woman's face caught a gleam
from the coming sunlight.   "Hope on! Hope on!"
It would yet be possible to get all the clothes out
before noon.

If she had looked into her neighbor's back gar-

den just then she would have
seen what the singer did.   A little brown bird was vainly peck-
ing away at a crust lying under
a tree.   Then the singer came,
with soft, quick steps, and broke
the crust into crumbs.   The sunlit hour had come for the bird.

"Broke the crust."

And it even came for Brother
George at dinner time.   Joy bells did not always
ring when he and Dorothy were in close quarters.
To-day his sister remarked, as she looked over his
shoulder at some exercise papers in his hands:
"What a nice writer you are, George.   Father

could n't write a bit better than that, I'm sure."

"Do n't you make fun of a fellow."

"I'm not.   I mean it."

It is strange, but true, words of praise do not often come in our way. The sunlight dazzled

George just at first, but when he had grown familiar with it, he called out just before going off to school again: "I say, Dorothy, do n't you go chop-ping that wood.   I'll do it when I come back again.   Wood chopping is n't in a girl's line."

"I mean it."

He even shut the door so quietly that the mother at work at her machine did not know that he had gone—the mother who had to work so many hours in order to make ends meet during the husband's long illness.   Her face looked very sad as she bent over her work, but such a change came over it as the door opened and the little housekeeper came in, bear-ing a cup of tea and a thin slice of bread and butter, laid daintily on a little tray.

"Why, Dorothy, what have you got there?"

"I'm not tired now.

"A cup of tea for you, mother, and you are to drink it, and to be sure to eat the bread and butter. I saw how little dinner you ate.   I was watching you, and you did look so very tired and worn."

"But I'm not tired now," said the mother, "not a bit of it. Why," lifting up her face from the teacup, "your loving care has strengthened me already."

"I shall be able to help you a lot after tea," said Dorothy, before returning to her kitchen duties.

As soon as they were over, and she had changed her dress, she peeped into her father's room to see if he was sleeping.

"Dear daddy," said she, stroking his white brow and smoothing the pillow, "you will soon be better now."

"The twenty-seventh Psalm."

"How does my little one know that?"

"Because the doctor generally goes away frowning, but to-day he actually had a smile on his face. "Daddy"—with a sudden movement, as though she had just thought of something—"shall I read you something? I have nothing to do before tea."

"Do, my darling."

The twenty-seventh Psalm was read in a soft, low voice.

The sick man's eyes were riveted on the reader's face. "Child, what made you read that Psalm?"

"Because, daddy, it's one of my favorites. Did you like it?"

"Yes." Then in a still lower voice, "I must tell you this, for God has been so good to me. I have prayed all day that He would send me some sign or message. And then you bring me words that have put new life into me. 'I had fainted, unless I had believed to see the goodness of the Lord in the land of the living.' 'Be strong, and let thine heart take courage.' Child," and there was a glad ring in the voice, "you have been doing angel's work."

Twilight was filling the valley when again the angels met. "How has your work fared to-day, companion?" asked the Angel of the Rainbow.

"My work has sped well to-day, for a girl in a lowly home, just along the path of her daily life, has helped me greatly. Ever so many times during the hours of light she has started, here and there, the sweet chiming bells of hope."

"Ah," said the Angel of the Rainbow, "now I understand how it was they sounded so much clearer to-day, and why my colors were so bright. Did you see the lovely bow I threw across from hill to hill, and then a second one, the rays gleaming all down the cliffs? Did they not make you think of the Rainbow round the Throne? It is only as I catch hope's glad singing rising from the byways below that I can paint my brightest colors."

ONE GIRL'S INFLUENCE

A YOUNG girl went from home," writes Mrs. Sangster, "to a large school where more than usual freedom of action and less than customary restraints were characteristics of the management. She found very little decided religious life there — an atmosphere, upon the whole, unfavorable to Christian culture. But she had given herself to the Lord, and she could live nowhere without letting her light shine.

"In a very short time she found two or three congenial spirits, more timid than herself, but equally devoted. A little prayer meeting began to be held once a week in her room. On Sabbaths in the afternoon, a few of the girls came together to study the Bible. Before the half year was over, the hallowed flame had swept from heart to heart, and there was a revival in that school."

"Yes, father, your dinner is ready."

TWO KINDS OF SERVICE

HAVE you put up my dinner, Maude?"
John Melvin asked the question almost
timidly. His daughter's face was clouded, her lips
were compressed, and she was making a great deal
of unnecessary noise as she moved about the
kitchen. She did not reply at once, and when
she spoke it was in no pleasant voice.

"Yes, father, your dinner is ready. Now I must
put up the children's dinners, and there is the iron-
ing to do, and I must do some cooking also. This
will be a busy day with me, but all my days seem
to be busy. Perhaps I do not understand how to
keep ahead of the work. I have no time for recreation; there seems to be nothing in life for me but
drudgery."

Mr. Melvin sighed heavily.

"I am sorry, Maude. If last season's crops had

not failed, I should have hired some stout woman to do the heavy work. It is too much for you, a girl of nineteen, to have all these cares; but what can I do?"

"You can do nothing, father, and no one is to blame. I expect to be a drudge. Amy," raising her voice, "where are you? Go and pick up the breakfast dishes, and be quick about it. It isn't time to get ready for school. Fred, what are you doing? Haven't I told you not to whistle in the kitchen? Oh, dear! one needs more patience than any mortal ever had!"

"I am sorry, Maude," said Mr. Melvin, again. "It was a sad day for us all when your mother died."

And then the discouraged man, old and worn before his time, took his dinner-pail and started for the distant wood-lot.

Maude continued to move rapidly about the kitchen and pantry, doing the morning's work and scolding the children in a shrill voice.

"What's the use of being so cross, Maude?" asked Amy, a bright-eyed girl of twelve. "I can't see that it does any good."

"I can't be so easy as you are, Amy. I wish things didn't fret me, but they do. And you have an easy time, while I have to work like a slave."

"I'm sure I help you all I can, Maude. I don't suppose you want me to stay out of school to work."

"You know I don't. You won't have time to

do any more this morning.   Now, Fred, I told you
to study hard to-day and not fail in your lessons."

"All right sis," rejoined Fred carelessly.

"Fred, how many times have I told you not to
call me 'Sis?' I am tired beyond endurance.   I
do n't want to hear another word from you this
morning, sir," she added as she saw the boy was
about to speak.

As the children left the house, Fred looked sig-
nifica..y at his sister.

"Was n't Maude cross this morning?   How she
did bang things!"

Amy puckered up her brow.

"I can't understand it, Fred.   Maude is always
scolding."

"Yes, and she belongs to the church.   I'm glad
I'm not a Christian, if she's one."

"Oh, hush, Fred!   Christian people are happier
than we are."

"Humph!   Maude professes to be a Christian,
but she can't be happy.   Seems to me she's the
unhappiest person I know.   Papa does n't belong
to the church, but he is n't always scolding."

"Well, I can't understand it," sighed Amy.
"But, Fred, you know mama was a Christian."

"She was a real Christian, too," said Fred so-
berly.   "But I guess it's hard work to be the real
thing.   Maude must be a make-believe one," he
added.

"Oh, hush, Fred!   I do n't like to hear you say
such things."

Left alone, Maude's hands were busy. At dinner time she ate a lunch, and at two o'clock was through her work.

"Everything's in order," she thought, as she looked about the neat kitchen. "And I'm not going to touch a bit of sewing this afternoon. I'll go into the sitting-room and rest until it's time to think about supper."

THE DREAM

In the pleasant little sitting-room Maude sat down in an easy rocker at the front window and looked out over the snow-covered fields. Presently she saw the bent form of a little old lady in a black coat and red hood coming up the path.

"Aunt Sarah Easler," she said to herself, "and coming here, too."

The old lady came in without knocking and Maude rose to meet her. Aunt Sarah seemed much agitated. She took both of the girl's hands in hers, tears streaming from her eyes.

"What is it, Aunt Sarah?" cried Maude. "Has anything happened?"

"My poor child! My poor child! May God help you!"

Maude felt herself growing faint, but she resolutely banished the feeling.

"What has happened?" she asked, in a voice so calm that it astonished herself. "The children?"

"The children are all right, my dear. It is your father."

"My father! What of him? Is he hurt?"

"Tired father? Supper's all ready."

The old lady bowed her head and replied in a broken voice: "Badly hurt, my dear."

"What is it, Aunt Sarah?"

Maude grasped Aunt Sarah's arm.

"Your face tells me that it is even worse than that," she said, calmly. "Is he dead?"

"My poor child!"

"You need say no more. I know he is."

Even as Maude spoke, she looked out of the window and saw four men bearing her father's form on a stretcher. She did not faint or cry out, but in a moment her mind went back over the three years that had passed since her mother's death, and she saw wherein she had failed as a daughter and sister.

Tears came to her relief, and as they gushed down over her cheeks she awoke with a start. She looked out of the window. Oh, thank God! no men were in sight, bearing her father's form on a stretcher.

"It was a dream," she murmured. "Heavenly Father, I thank thee!" And she formed a few resolutions and lifted up her heart in prayer for help.

"How terribly I have erred and wandered from the way," she said aloud. "This dream has opened my eyes, and I see what I have been doing. What must have papa thought of me? No wonder that he is not a Christian. I have wondered, too, that the children have been so indifferent to religious teaching, but the influence of my life has spoiled everything. But, thank God! the present is mine, my dear ones are spared to me, and henceforth I will strive to have my life count for Christ."

When the children came that night they looked in wonder at their sister. There was a smile on her face, and her voice was gentle when she spoke to them. The tea-table was neatly spread and Fred saw his favorite hot rolls. Presently Mr. Melvin came in, somewhat timidly, expecting as usual to hear complaints and impatient exclamations from Maude. Instead, she greeted him pleasantly.

"Tired, father? Supper's ready. I've made some of the toast you like and opened a can of peaches.

"I suppose you are very tired, Maude," said Mr. Melvin, looking wonderingly at his daughter.

"I'm a little tired, father, but I'm thankful for the privilege of getting tired. I have a comfortable home, and we are all in good health. You see, father, I am beginning to count my blessings. I have been a fault-finding, ungrateful girl, and have made you all unhappy; but I hope to make some amends for the past."

"God bless you, my daughter!" said John Melvin, huskily.

DUTY AND PLEASURE

"DUTY first, and pleasure afterward," wrote Amy Leslie in her copy-book one fine morning.

Line after line she penned, making many a mistake, for her thoughts were far away. At last her mother, who was sitting near her, said, "Amy, this is the third time you have spelled pleasure without a 'p,' and left out the 'f' in afterward. Put down your pen and tell me what you are thinking about; for I am sure it is not of your copy."

"I was only thinking," replied Amy, "how glad I should be if my copy said, 'Pleasure first—duty afterward.' It is very hard always to have the disagreeable part first. I wish I could have one whole week with no duties at all! How I should enjoy myself!"

Mrs. Leslie remained silent for a moment; then she said, while a quiet smile played round her lips, "Well, Amy, for once you shall have what you want. For a whole week you may amuse yourself; no duties, mind, my child,—none at all."

"There is no chance of my wanting any, I assure you, mama," said Amy, joyfully; "I shall be so happy, you'll see!"

"Very well, then," said Mrs. Leslie; "you may begin to-morrow. To-day I shall expect you to do as usual."

Amy said no more; she finished her copy, learned her lessons, then went to the nursery to take charge of her little brother while the nurse was busy with other work. Afterward there were socks to mend, and an errand to run, and buttons to sew on to baby's shoes, and a letter to write. And so the day passed, and the next morning dawned on our pleasure-loving little friend.

"No duties" she said to herself, as she woke at seven, which was her usual time for rising; "so I can lie in bed as long as I please." She turned over, and as she could not sleep, began making plans for the day, and thinking what a delightful time she would have. About half past nine she came down stairs, to find her breakfast on the table; milk, toast, and egg, all as cold as possible. "What a wretched breakfast!" she said, as she took her seat.

"Well, dear," replied Mrs. Leslie, "your breakfast was ready at the usual time, and of course is cold now."

Amy said no more. She ate with only half her usual appetite, and, finishing in about five minutes put away her chair, and left the room. As she went up stairs to fetch her hat, baby in the nursery stretched his arms for her to take him; but she hurried past, and left the little fellow crying with disappointment.

Soon she came down again, with a fairy book in one hand, and a box of chocolate drops in the other. The sweets had been a present, but hitherto her mother had allowed her to have only one or two daily; now, however, she might do as she liked, and at present her idea of perfect bliss was the combined charms of chocolate drops and fairy stories.

"Carried it like a baby."

For about two hours she sat in the garden; then she grew tired, and a little sick from eating too much chocolate, and was returning to the house, when her pet kitten ran out to meet her. For a short time she amused herself by playing with it, dressing it up in her pocket handkerchief and carrying it like a baby; but Miss Pussy wearied of this, and at last jumped out of her new dress and her mistress' arms, leaving a scratch as a keepsake behind her.

Altogether, the morning was hardly a successful

one, nor was the afternoon much better. After
dinner, one of Amy's little sisters tore her dress,
and was running to Amy to ask her to mend it;
but Mrs. Leslie said: —

"Don't go to your sister, my child, come to me;"
and little Jessie, wondering, let her mother darn the
rent. Amy felt very uncomfortable, for she knew
that Mrs. Leslie's eyes were not strong, and were
probably aching with the effort of such fine work;
but she shrank from offering her services, and made
her escape from the room as soon as she could.

In the evening she was about to draw her chair
to the fire and read the newspaper to Mr. Leslie, a
duty of which she had always felt rather proud;
but her father gravely took the paper out of her
hand, saying quickly, "No, Amy, this is a duty;
remember you are to amuse yourself and do nothing
else."

Amy's eyes filled with tears, and she ran up
stairs to her own room. She had no heart to read
the fairy book, or to make clothes for her doll, or to
play with the kitten, or even to eat the rest of her
chocolate drops.

"I shall never be able to bear another day of
this," she said to herself; "I thought it would be
so delightful to have no duties, but somehow my
play does not seem half so good as it did before."

The next day brought no real pleasure and comfort. Listlessly Amy wandered about, having no
zest for any of her former amusements, and feeling
thoroughly unhappy. She began to long for the

very duties which had seemed so irksome to her; she could hardly keep from tears when she saw others busy over lessons, or her mother doing work which had formerly been hers.

At last her misery ended in a fit of crying, and shutting herself up in her own room, she gave way to it. Sob followed sob so quickly that she did not hear her door open, until her mother's arms were round her, and her hot, aching head was pillowed on her mother's shoulder. Not a word passed between them for a few minutes; then Amy sobbed out, "O mother! mother! the copy was quite right, 'Duty first, and pleasure afterward;' for without duty there is no pleasure at all."

"Her mother's arms were around her."

"Do tell us a story."

THE DANGEROUS DOOR

OH, cousin Will, do tell us a story! There's just time before the school-bell rings." And Harry, Kate, Bob, and little Peace crowded about their older cousin until he declared himself ready to do anything they wished.

"Very well," said Cousin Will. "I will tell you about some dangerous doors I have seen."

"Oh, that's good!" exclaimed Bob. "Were they all iron and heavy bars? And if one passed in, did they shut and keep them there forever?"

"No; the doors I mean are pink or scarlet, and when they open you can see a row of little servants standing all in white, and behind them is a little lady dressed in crimson."

"What? That's splendid!" cried Kate. "I should like to go in myself."

[208]

"Ah! it is what comes out of these doors that makes them so dangerous. They need a strong guard on each side, or else there is great trouble."

"Why, what comes out?" said little Peace, with wondering eyes.

"When the guards are away," said Cousin Will, "I have known some things to come out sharper than arrows, and they make terrible wounds. Quite lately I saw two pretty little doors, and one opened and the little lady began to talk like this: 'What a stuck-up thing Lucy Waters is! And did you see that horrid dress made out of her sister's old one?' 'Oh, yes,' said the other little crimson lady from the other door, 'and what a turned-up nose she has!' Then poor Lucy, who was around the corner, ran home and cried all evening."

"I know what you mean," cried Kate, coloring.

"Were you listening?"

"Oh, you mean our mouths are doors!" exclaimed Harry, "and the crimson lady is Miss Tongue; but who are the guards, and where do they come from?"

"You may ask the Great King. This is what you must say: 'Set a watch, O Lord, before my mouth: keep the door of my lips.' Then He will send Patience to stand on one side and Love on the other, and no unkind word will dare come out."

THE GOLDEN WINDOWS

OH, dear!" exclaimed Ruth impatiently, as she put the library to rights. "I do wish we could have a new carpet this spring. I never liked this at all, and now it is so faded and worn it is simply dreadful. It makes me miserable every time I look at it."

"Then, since you say you cannot very well have a new one just now, why do you look at it?" asked Aunt Rachel, smiling. "There are a great many unpleasant things in our lives — we find them every day — some of which we are unable to prevent. If we persist in thinking of them and keep fretting about them, we make ourselves and everybody about us miserable.

"It seems to me we might all learn a lesson from the bees. I have read that when anything objectionable that they are unable to remove gets into a hive, they set to work immediately to cover it all over with wax. They just shut it up in an air-tight cell, and then forget all about it. Is n't that a wise way for us to manage with our vexations and troubles?

"Someone sent me a postal the other day with this motto: 'The secret of happiness is not in do-ing what one likes, but in liking what one has to

do.' It is not in having and doing just as we like, but in being deter-mined to make the best of the inevitable. When you find an unpleasant thing in your life that cannot be removed, learn to seal it up and forget it.

"And then I think that many times it helps to get a different view of things. You remember the fable of the golden windows, do you not? A little boy who had very few pretty things in his own home because his parents were poor, used often to stand in his own doorway at sunset time and look longingly at the big house at the top of the oppos-ite hill. Such a wonderful house as it was! Its windows were all of gold, which shone so bright that it often made his eyes blink to look at them. 'If only our house was as beautiful,' he would say. 'I would not mind wearing patched clothes and having only bread and milk for supper.'

"One afternoon his father told him he might do just as he pleased, so he trudged down the hill

from his house and up the other long hill.   He was
going to see the golden windows.   But when he
reached the top of the other hill he stopped in dis-
may ; his lips began to quiver, his eyes filled with
tears.   There were no golden
windows there—nothing but
plain, common windows like
his own.   'I thought you had
beautiful golden windows in
your house,' he said to the little girl in the yard.

"'Oh, no!' she said; 'our
windows are n't worth looking
at, but stand beside me and you
will see a lovely house with
truly golden windows.   See?'
The little boy looked.   'Why,

"A lovely house with truly golden windows."

that is my house,' he said, 'and I never knew we had golden windows!'

"You see, much depends on your point of view.

"I have lived to be an old woman, my dear, and I have come to feel that the most heroic lives are lived by those who put their own vexations and troubles out of sight, and strive by every means in their power to ease the burden of the world; who leave always behind them the influence of a brave, cheery, loving spirit."

TRUST ALWAYS: NEVER FRET

Trust in the Lord, and do good;
Dwell in the land, and follow after faithfulness:
Delight thyself also in the Lord;
And He shall give thee the desires of thine heart.

Commit thy way unto the Lord,
Trust also in Him,
And He shall bring it to pass.
And He shall make thy righteousness to go forth as the light,
And thy judgment as the noonday.

Rest in the Lord,
And wait patiently for Him:
Fret not thyself because of him who prospereth in his way,
Because of the man who bringeth wicked devices to pass.
Cease from anger, and forsake wrath:
Fret not thyself; it tendeth only to evil-doing.

PSALM 37 : 3-8.

"The light of the sun does us no good unless we are living in it!"

THE NEW LIFE

THE light of the sun does us no good unless we are living in it! Yes, that is just what the minister said," mused Tim, as he tossed his Sabbath-school paper upon the table, and gave himself up to the flow of his own thoughts. "Yes, he said just that, and more, too. He said that the life of Christ will do us little good unless we are living in it; that is, unless we are Christians, it makes little difference to us whether Christ gave His life for us or not."

"What is on your mind, now?" It was Tim's sister Ada who asked this question as she came running into the room upon her return from school. She had stopped on her way to gather violets, and that, you see, is why she had not reached home as soon as Tim.

"Oh, I was just thinking about what the minis-

[214]

ter said last Sabbath, that is all," replied the lad in a low voice.

"Oh, yes, what he said about people being 'born again' if they would live the Christ life, and that reminds me that I must write his text down in my text book. Let's see, it was last Christmas, was n't it, when Mrs. Martin gave us those little books, and told us to write in them the text of every sermon we heard preached ; and I am glad to say that I have not missed many Sabbaths since then."

"Neither have I," said Tim. "And do you know, I have been wondering whether Mrs. Martin will give her class any presents this Christmas."

"Oh, I don't know. I should think a teacher did her duty by teaching a Sabbath-school class fifty-two times in a year, without spending her money on presents for us, even if we are but four. I think it would be more appropriate for us to be giving her a present this year, than for us to be expecting one from her."

"And let's get up one for her," proposed Tim.

"And that means that we will," laughed Ada. "When you say, 'let's' in that tone something is always sure to happen."

"But we don't want to have the whole say about the presents ourselves," observed the boy, evidently pleased at his sister's compliment. "Mark and Nettie have n't come by from school yet. When they do, we will call them in, and see what can be done."

"All right, and let's watch for them."

The windows facing the road were immediately taken possession of, and it was not long before Ada and Tim were both rapping on the panes of glass.

"What is it?" shouted Mark from the road.

"Come and see," replied Ada.

Mark and Nettie, a rosy-cheeked brother and sister, were soon in the little sitting-room, and Ada and Tim were laying before them their plans for Christmas.

"It is just like this," said Ada; "I found Tim dreaming about Christmas, and I just suggested that we give Mrs. Martin a Christmas present this year. Now what do you think of it?"

"That would be just the thing," said Nettie.

"But what do you think she would want?" queried Mark.

"We can't tell, unless we ask her," replied Ada. "But have any of us ever heard her say what she wanted?"

"I have," said Tim. "I have heard her say that what she wanted the most of anything was to have her scholars come to Christ."

"But I mean something that we could give her."

"But if we should make up our minds to be Christians, it would make her pleased," said Tim, "and perhaps she'd rather be pleased in this way than to have a present."

"I know that she would," said Nettie; "and I say, let's settle the question once for all."

The others looked in amazement at Nettie; they could scarcely understand what she meant. Her face was flushed, and she was trembling with emotion, but one thing was certain, and that was that Nettie was in earnest—also Tim; and whatever Tim wanted the others to do they generally did.

"You may as well tell us what you do mean," said Mark.

"Why, just what I said," replied Tim. "I think it is about time that we began to think some of being Christians—that is, if what the minister says is true, and I suppose that it is, for everybody believes everything else that he says, when he has anything to say in our house and in the store."

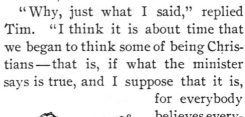

"We might sign a paper."

"I should say as much," said Nettie.

"But what can be done about it?" queried Mark, in perplexity.

"We might all sign a paper, telling her what we intend to do, and give it to her Christmas," proposed Tim.

"So we can," said Mark, "and let's do it at once."

So Tim went to the desk, and spent a few minutes writing something upon a piece of paper. When he had finished, he turned around and asked: "Want to hear it?"

"Of course," answered Nettie.

So he read: "We four scholars of your class have made up our minds to be Christians, and we give you this information as your Christmas remembrance from us."

"Just the thing," said Ada.

"And I suppose that we must all sign it," suggested Nettie.

"Of course," answered Tim.

"But is this all that we must do to be Christians?" queried Mark.

"I should say not," answered Tim, "but if Mrs. Martin knows that we are in earnest, she will tell us what to do."

So the paper was signed by the four, after which Mark and Nettie continued on their way homeward.

On the Sabbath following Christmas, after the class had gathered, and were waiting for Sabbath-school to begin in the little church on the hill, Tim passed to Mrs. Martin an envelope bearing her name. When she opened it and read the note that was within, her eyes filled with tears of joy.

"Oh, my precious class! My precious class!" This was all she could say, as she looked from one to another with face shining like an angel's.

"We thought that you'd tell us just what to do," began Ada. "We felt that we needed help from you."

"And you shall have it this very hour. We will let the lesson go to-day, and just have a little meeting all to ourselves."

"That will be just beautiful!" exclaimed Nettie.

While the other classes in the church were discussing the lesson for the day, Mrs. Martin's class in the pew in the rear were settling the great question of their lives.

Mrs. Martin began by telling them the story of the Christ—how Christ left His heavenly home, and came to earth to die for all men, since all are sinners; and how all may be saved from sin by being sorry for their wrong-doing, deciding to lead a right life, and taking Him as their personal Saviour. "Is this what you all believe?"

"It is," replied the class, softly.

Then all closed their eyes, and Mrs. Martin prayed softly for them, after which each prayed for pardon, and by the time Sabbath-school was dismissed, all felt that Christ had accepted them as His very own.

"Oh, how I shall prize this little note," said Mrs. Martin, as they were leaving the church for home. "You could not have given me a Christmas remembrance which would have meant more to me. And I am sure that I am not the only one you have remembered this day—you have given yourselves to Christ, who died and arose from the grave for you, and He will treasure the Christmas gift you have given Him more than I can the one you have given me."

THE IMPOSSIBLE YESTERDAY

SHE was a tiny girl, playing by herself in a wide, grassy yard. The older children had gone to school, but she, too young for that, was busying herself with putting in order a playhouse in an arbor—arranging it as nearly as possible as it had been the day before, when she and two or three little mates had enjoyed such a merry time there. To and fro trudged the tireless feet, patiently the small hands worked, and at last all was complete. Then the young worker looked about her, and slowly a shadow of disappointment crept over the face that had been so eager. Something was lacking. Everything was in the remembered order, but it did not seem the same. She studied it for a minute or two, then walked away and sat down on a sunny doorstep. The mother found her there a little later, a listless, quiet little figure.

"Are you tired of your playhouse already, dear?" she asked.

The childish eyes were uplifted with a look of wistful wonder in them, and the answer came slowly.

"I can't do it—I can't make yesterday over again."

It was the hopeless task that in one form or another we all undertake, and with which many darken their whole lives because they will not learn that it is an impossible one. Yesterday's roses died with the day, yesterday's manna was only for yesterday's need, but there are new flowers and new food for to-day from the same gracious hand that bestowed the other, if only we will go

"I can't make yesterday over again."

cheerfully and trustingly forward. The treasures and pleasures we have had are for memory and thanksgiving, but the moment we sit down beside them to grieve or to try to reconstruct them out of their ruins we have changed them from a blessing to a hindrance. We cannot make yesterday over again.

A CHILD'S PUZZLE

MEG had been playing in the garden all the morning, and when mama called her in she had earth on her hands, and smuts on her face, and she looked such a grubby little thing.

Mama smiled. "You have been having a good time, Meg," she said.

And she put a tin bason with some soap and warm water in it on a chair where Meg could reach.

"Now, then, wash your hands and face, dear. Dada will soon be in for dinner."

But Meg pouted. "I don't want to wash," she said. "I am not dirty."

Mama waited a little, but when she saw that Meg did not begin to wash, she said, quite gravely:

"You cannot sit at the table, as you are, dear. If you do not wash, then you must go without your dinner."

Meg stood a minute, then, as she saw that mama

was quite firm, she put her hands into the water and began to wash and scrub them.

Lucy is older than Meg, and she had looked on all the time to see what Meg would do. When Lucy Lucy saw her begin to wash and be good, she said:—

"Why is it, mama, that you and dada can do just as you like about everything, but we children have to do as you tell us all the time? I don't think it is fair. I wish we could do as we like, too."

Mama did not speak for a moment. In her heart she said, "Lord help me to make this plain to my little girls."

"Did Meg have to wash?" she asked them.

"Yes," said Lucy. "If not, she would have to—"

"Bear the punishment," said mama. "You say, Lucy, that dada and I do just what we choose, and that is quite true. But if we choose to do wrong, then we have to be punished too, and the punishment is far worse than any that dada or I can give you, for it comes from God.

"Little children do not always know right from wrong, so in order to help them and make right easy, God gives them parents and teachers to praise them when they are good"—and here mama laid her hand on Meg's head—"or else to punish them when they are naughty.

"My two little girls may do just as they choose, as long as they choose to do what is right, and then when they are big and there is no mama to tell them all the time what to do, I hope they will do right of themselves."

HOW ONE GIRL SHOWED THAT SHE WAS SORRY

IN a little village lived a poor old woman with a pretty granddaughter. One day the aged woman went out without her crutch, but her granddaughter was near to serve her as a support. It continued thus for a long time. To the promenade, to church, or market, the good old grandame no longer used her crutch, but leaned on her granddaughter. There was much prattling about this in the village, and all wondered. At last they found out the cause. The granddaughter, in a fit of passion, threw her grandmother's crutch in the fire, and the old woman was too poor to buy another. The hasty girl cried and repented, and the frail old woman pardoned her; but, to make reparation, her grandchild never quitted her for an instant, and served as a faithful crutch, till she saved up money enough to buy a substantial new crutch, on which were these words, "Repentance and restoration."